I dedicate this book to my wife, best friend, and partner-in-crime in this crazy life, Joanna Weaver Puckett. Thank you for always believing in me and standing strong by my side. I love you.

Hell Is For Real, Too!

By: Jim Puckett

Chapter 1   Am I in Hell?

I died on January 16, 2010 in a Medivac helicopter as I was being rushed to Doctor's Hospital in Augusta, GA. I didn't stay dead, but I clinically died. My heart stopped beating, and my lungs stopped breathing. My near death experience didn't include angels singing, trumpets blaring or a bright white light at the end of a tunnel. Not even close. No, what I remember is dark, murky, cold water….The deep dirty water was nearly up to my chin, and, as I looked around, I realized I was with a bunch of other people I didn't want to be with. It was so incredibly dark, definitely nighttime, but there were people as far as I could see in the water. We were all enclosed in some kind of giant fence or something similar that was actually down in the water. My feet weren't touching the bottom. I realized right away that no one could get out. I just remember struggling to keep my head above the water. The people around me were definitely not friendly. They were mean and agitated and wanted to fight. I somehow knew this was an evil place with a lot of bad people who wanted to hurt me or at the very least sure weren't interested in helping me. I remember wanting to get out of there worse than anything I'd ever wanted before. I remember a sense of complete helplessness and despair and sheer terror. There was absolutely nothing I could do to get out. There was nowhere to go! I was terrified...more so than I had ever been in my life. I was SO confused. What had happened to get me to this awful place? Why was I here? Where was my family? How will I ever get out of here? Am I stuck here forever? Those were the questions running at breakneck speed through my mind. People were yelling at each other and trying to get out. The faces around me in the water continued to get even more menacing and threatening. I tried my best to avoid any and all eye contact while I tried to sort things out. They were grabbing and shaking the fence, but there was obviously no way out. I was too scared to move or speak except for trying to keep my head above water. I kept trying stay out of everyone's way and not draw any attention to myself. I was so confused because I had no memory of how I got there. The fear I experienced in that water was something I never want to feel again. I thought my life was over, and I was doomed to stay in that water for eternity. So....what did I do? I did the only thing I knew to do. The only thing that had been instilled in me since childhood that you were supposed to do when you needed help. I prayed....and I prayed and I prayed and I prayed. I bowed my head, trying to keep the water from going in my mouth, and I talked to God. I asked for another chance. I cried. I asked to go back to my family. I'm not sure exactly what my words were, but I promised to be a better Christian and a better husband and a better father and a better everything else. But you see, the thing was….I meant every single word coming from my mouth. I somehow knew that the only sliver of hope I had to get out of that dark evil water was prayer. And then I woke up…

Chapter 2 – Waking Up

My beautiful and witty (i.e. smarty-pants) wife Joanna and I have differing memories of what my first words were after I woke up in the ICU Burn Unit at Doctor's Hospital in Augusta, GA from a two month long medically induced coma... I KNOW for a fact that my first words to her must have been "I love you, baby". "It's so good to see your face." She loves to tell everyone the obviously made up story that my first words were, " I missed the Super Bowl, didn't I?!!" I think the truth lies somewhere in the middle. I do recall that as Joanna and several other family members were gathering around to celebrate my awakening, I groggily noticed that they all had the same white shirts on which said Puckett Prayer Warrior on the front. I just remember thinking to myself, "Uh oh, I must have been here a REALLY long time if they've already had shirts made up!"

Chapter 3 – The Explosion

On January 16, 2010, a plastic red gasoline container exploded on me on our back patio in Cordele, GA. I had been attempting to light some wood in a wrought iron outdoor fireplace. You know...one of those $99 deals you get at Lowe's or Home Depot. I always used Duraflame starter logs, but I had forgotten to pick one up at WalMart earlier in the day. My wife and I were going to sit outside and check out the eclipse on the long Martin Luther King weekend. But I couldn't get the dang fire started. I tried kindling, wadded up paper towels, straw...nothing worked. So once I had a very small flame barely burning, I went around to my garage and grabbed the small red gas can I used for summer mowing. It only had a little leftover gas in it. I figured I'd just splash a tiny bit on the little flame, and everything would be great. We'd have a nice roaring fire for our relaxing night outside. I've done this countless times before without an issue. Little did I know that under the right conditions, a flame can ignite the fumes from the gasoline and shoot the flame back into the gas can at which time the gas can will explode on you. Which is exactly what happened to me. I stood over the fireplace and splashed a very small amount of gas on the tiny flame. And yes, the gas can violently and nearly fatally exploded on me. My wife and neighbors would later tell me how incredibly loud the BOOM of the explosion was. Ironically, I never heard it. All I remember hearing was a loud SWOOSH and then seeing nothing but bright orange flames in front of my eyes. I distinctly remember somewhat calmly thinking, "Oh crap...I'm on fire." Stop, drop, and roll never occurred to me, and several firefighters later told me that had I tried that maneuver, I most certainly would have died right there rolling around in my backyard. When you have an accelerant like gasoline all over you stop, drop, and roll apparently won't get the job done. Luckily for me, my first instinct was to turn and run as fast as I could and jump in the small pond which separated my back yard from the first fairway of Pine Hills Golf Course. It's probably twenty yards from my patio to the pond, and I'm quite sure I covered it in record time. My son Luke often doubts my speed, but it's amazing how fast your feet can carry you when you're on fire. I'm not sure how many of our neighbors saw me, but I can't help but try to picture their astonished faces as a 6'4" 250 lb ball of fire shot across the yard and dove head first into the pond at nearly midnight. I tell my wife and kids that I must have looked like the superhero The Flash, but they just laugh and say it was probably more like Will Ferrell's underwear-clad jog down Main Street in the movie "Old School" – except I was on fire. Really? I don't get it. Anyway, I remember going under the water and literally hearing the sizzling sound as the dirty pond water quenched the fire and saved my life. I then thought to myself, "Ok, you can get up now." As I walked out of the pond, I recall thinking that if I wasn't already dead, Joanna was going to kill me. She had often warned me not to do that (the gas on the fire thing), but nooo...I knew what I was doing! Way to go, knucklehead. I stumbled around the house to the garage knowing that I probably had to go to the local hospital. I remember looking down at my hands and seeing skin dripping from them. It definitely wasn't a pretty sight. Not to mention that the explosion had apparently burned all of my clothes off, and my big butt was standing in my driveway, all burned up and naked as could be.   About that time, our neighbor, a registered nurse, walked up to me and wrapped a blanket around me. I apologized to her for being naked, and I told her I had to go to the hospital. She said, "No, you have to go to the Augusta Burn Center." I didn't know it at the time, but she and her husband David had jumped into action as soon as they heard the explosion. And most likely saved my life. David, a lifelong paramedic, had an ambulance on the way in minutes and had notified our local MediVac helicopter that their services were going to be needed to save a life tonight. The next and last thing I remember before I woke up two months later was being wheeled into an ambulance on a gurney, seeing my wife crying hysterically and telling her that I was sorry and that I loved her. She told me that she loved me, and then I guess I was out.

Chapter 4 - Here for a Reason

Seems very few people outside my family and close friends expected me to survive my accident. Remember David the paramedic, my neighbor? On the day I got home 2 ½ months later after being released from the hospital, he and his wife sat in my living room, and he just kept staring at me with this dazed look on his face. As we talked, he just simply said, "Jim, when we put you on that helicopter, I thought you only had a one-way ticket to Augusta, buddy. I never expected to see you alive again." After I woke up, people kept telling me that I was a walking talking miracle. They kept saying that God kept me here for a reason. I don't think any of them knew exactly what it was; nor did I. And maybe I still don't? This may sound crazy, but from the minute I woke up, I couldn't wait to get started with the rest of my life. At the time, I was the assistant principal at Ben Hill Elementary School. I had 750 third, fourth, and fifth graders and a staff of amazing teachers to get back to. While still laying in the hospital with a trach in my neck, one of the very first things I told Joanna was that I wanted to write a book and become a motivational speaker. I can't explain to you why. I just knew that was going to be my life's calling from then on.

Maybe my burning desire to write comes from my love of reading. I've always been a much more than avid reader. When I was a young boy growing up in Smyrna, GA, I can remember reading literally everything I could find. I'd go by the old wooden bookshelf in our living room and grab a big blue Encyclopedia Britannica before going into the bathroom. I'd just open it to a random page and read for the duration of my stay. Weird, right? Sometimes I'd grab a cereal box from the kitchen and read all about how Captain Crunch was stocked full of vitamins and minerals for the young and young at heart. If I forgot reading material, I'd read the back of my Dad's shaving cream or my Mom's hand lotion or the label of whatever toothpaste had been on sale that week. The Hardy Boys and Nancy Drew were the first "real" books I remember. I devoured every one I could get my hands on. Then it was comic books. I wasn't a big superhero guy, though. I loved The Archies and especially Richie Rich. By the way, here I am trying to write the early chapters of my first book and just had to stop because my 11 year old daughter Hannah had to come in and give me a hug. "How's the book coming, Daddy?" I just started ten minutes ago!

So for more than five years now, I've planned to write my story. I just never could wrap my head around exactly what I wanted to say. Lying in bed one night, it just started coming to me. I nearly got up in the middle of the night to start writing. I knew I wanted to share my experience with others – the ups and downs of my recovery, but I want it to be much more than that. I want to inspire. I want to motivate. I want to make you laugh. I want to introduce you to my family, my friends, and many of my students and players. I want to share with you not only the details of my accident, but how it shaped me into a better person. A better husband, a better father, a better Christian. I do not have all the answers to this crazy wonderful life we live, but I do think I can help you find them.

So for more than two months, I laid in a hospital bed at the J.M. Still Burn Center in Doctor's Hospital in Augusta, GA. I was 42 years old and an assistant principal at Ben Hill Elementary School in my hometown of Fitzgerald, GA. I had a beautiful wife, Joanna, and two amazing children. My son Luke was a junior in high school, and daughter Hannah was in first grade. When I woke up from the coma, I was understandably on many medications. Painkillers, antidepressants, antibiotics, etc. So my mind was obviously still a little foggy. Unfortunately, one of the first things I remember was visiting with my wife and my younger brother Wayne. Wayne was sitting on one side of my bed, and my wife was sitting on the other. Wayne was about to leave and go back to his home in Thomaston, GA. In my drug induced stupor, I became convinced that my wife Joanna was going to either kill me or have me killed that day. Each time she turned her head, I would plead with my brother not to leave me because she was going to kill me. Wayne said, "Jim, that's silly. No one is going to kill you. I'll call you tonight." I hysterically replied, "You can't call me tonight because I'll be dead!" I begged and begged him not to leave me. I was seriously terrified. I believed with all my heart that I wouldn't live through the night because my wife was going to kill me. Luckily, Joanna had been warned that paranoia was a side effect of some of the drugs I was taking so she took it all with a grain of salt. I was literally yelling (as much as you can yell with a trach tube in your throat) at a security guard in the hallway to get someone to help me. I remember being so furious at my brother and absolutely couldn't believe that he was just going to leave and let Joanna kill me. The scary thing is that I believed with all my heart and soul that my best friend in the world was going to kill me. We all laugh about it now, but it definitely reinforced my conviction to NEVER take any mind altering drugs of any kind. Crazy!

Joanna had been a Deputy Sheriff in metro Atlanta before we moved south to Cordele in November of 2008. After working her entire adult life, we made the decision for her to be a stay-at-home Mom with our daughter Hannah. We thought it would be worth the loss in income for her to be with Hannah each day. Looking back now, that was one of the best decisions we have ever made. More on that later though.

Let me share a little more about my family with you. My wife Joanna and I were married July 10, 2000. It was the second marriage for both of us. I had a son Luke from my first marriage. Luke was seven when we got married. Joanna has adored him from the day she met him. She has always treated him like her own son, and that was just one of many reasons I fell in love with her. Joanna is a 5'10' beautiful redhead. She has a zest for life that is infectious to all who meet her. She laughs loud and lives loud. So at the time of my accident, Joanna, Hannah, and I lived in our home at Pine Hills Golf Course in Cordele, GA. My mother and her husband John live in Fitzgerald, GA – about 30 miles from Cordele. My Daddy, Jimmy Puckett, passed away at the age of 43 in a car accident. Fitzgerald is my hometown. Also in Fitzgerald are my younger sister Susie Salinas and her husband Roland. My brother Wayne and his wife Karen live in Thomaston, GA with their three children.

Chapter 5 - The Plan

I shared with you where all of my family members lived at the time of my accident so that you would better understand "the plan". What most people don't understand about an accident like mine, especially when the patient (me!), is in a prolonged coma is that the family members go through many more hardships than the patient. After all, I was asleep. By the time I awoke, I had gone through about seventeen different surgeries. Skin grafts, lung cleansings, blood transfusions and more. When I arrived by way of medivac helicopter at Doctor's Hospital, the "plan" was already beginning to materialize. Understand that my family is one of those families that always stand by each other no matter what. Whether you have a sprained ankle or 65% of your body is covered in 2nd and 3rd degree burns, we will be there for you. All of us! As family and friends began to gather in the hospital, my brother, at some point, stated emphatically, "Even though Jim is in a coma, I don't want him to ever be alone in this hospital – not for a minute." "One of us will always be here." Joanna was probably in shock at this point. The plan became that Joanna would stay with me each week from Monday afternoon until Thursday afternoon. She would then leave and drive 3 ½ hours home to Cordele to be with our daughter Hannah through Monday. From Monday through Thursday, Hannah would stay with our close friends across the street in Cordele, Robin and Keith Carter, so that she could continue with school. Their daughter Somer was Hannah's best friend. My wife wanted Hannah's life to continue as normally as possible through this ordeal. My sister Susie would leave her job as the controller of Dorminy Medical Center in Fitzgerald on Thursdays at noon and travel to Augusta. She would be with me by herself until Friday when the rest of my family would begin to arrive each week. Just as Joanna was there all week, my son Luke, sister Susie, my Mom, and stepfather John were there every weekend throughout my ordeal. My brother Wayne, his wife Karen, and their family were there as much as possible as well. They would all take turns visiting me in the ICU during visiting hours...just watching me all plugged up to machines and sleeping. They made sure that I was never ever left alone. They read to me, talked to me, and decorated my room with pictures and well-wishing cards. My wife even connected to an old classmate and friend of mine Manon Wingate, who happened to live in Augusta. Even though I hadn't seen or spoken to Manon since graduating in 1985, she befriended Joanna like she's known her forever. Talk about finding out who your true friends are...I can barely write about Manon and her mother Oma without getting choked up. Oma stayed with me the very few times when my family members were in transition and no one could be there for a few hours. Everyone was sticking to the plan – the plan to never leave me alone in the hospital.

It definitely threw everyone's lives into a tailspin, but they did what close families do. They made it work. And I will be forever grateful that they did. We couldn't have done it without help though. The hospital provided a free apartment for my wife to stay in during the week. A local church provided housing for my other family members during the weekends. Joanna will tell you really quickly that having her own space to go to at night helped her stay sane throughout this ordeal.

Chapter 6 – Coming to Grips

Upon waking from the coma, as happy as I was to be awake and to just be alive, coming to grips with the reality of my situation was tough. I had always prided myself on staying in excellent shape. I had lifted weights on a regular basis since high school and college. Taking care of my body was very important to me. In fact, doctors said that me being in such good shape prior to my accident is probably why I'm still alive today. So, being a somewhat vain man married to a strikingly beautiful woman, one of my first thoughts was "What if I'm so horribly disfigured that my wife wants nothing to do with me anymore?" I knew I was obviously burned badly, but no one was telling me how badly. I knew I had a lot of bandages on my arms and legs and feet. Doctors and nurses would come in and change dressings and look at my injuries and talk among themselves. I don't think they wanted me to know how bad it was, or they just thought I was so out of it that I wouldn't comprehend. I remember it took several days after waking up before I dared to touch my face. I had no idea how badly burned it was, and no one had said anything. So one night while lying in bed trying to watch TV, I tried to muster the courage to touch my face. It was probably 2 or 3 in the morning (It's nearly impossible to sleep in ICU at night!) Nurses and doctors are forever coming in and switching on the insanely bright overhead lights without warning. It's hard to explain, but I was on so many drugs that even bringing my hand to my face was a chore. I remember finally bringing my right hand and touching my right cheek. I'm not sure what I expected, but what I felt made no sense. I expected rough scarred skin, but instead I felt these tiny raised thingies coming out of my face. I know thingies isn't very descriptive, but I can't describe it any other way. Kind of like the dimples on a golf ball or basketball but much rougher? I remember rubbing my entire face with that hand, and just thinking that I must look like a monster. I'm pretty sure I cried a little, but I really don't remember that well. I do recall that when my nurse came in soon after, she asked why I kept rubbing my face. I told her I was trying to figure out what these "thingies" were on my face. She just laughed and said, "Mr. Puckett, that's just your beard stubble!" We need to shave you!" I didn't believe her so she asked if I wanted to see a mirror? "No!, I said adamantly. "No mirrors!" Since waking up, I had purposefully stayed away from looking into a mirror. I was terrified at what I might see. My wife Joanna, who's just full of jokes, loves to tell people that it's ironic that I stay away from mirrors now because before my accident, I never walked by a mirror without looking at myself. (Her story – not mine) There's probably a smidgen of truth to that statement, if I'm being honest. Anyway, the nurse finally convinced me that it was just my beard I was feeling. She lathered my face up, shaved me with one of those little blue plastic hospital razors, and told me, " Now feel your face." I very slowly and carefully brought my hand back to my face. It was smooth! The thingies were gone! Thank you God! One of my many small victories. She again offered me a mirror, and I again politely refused.

You must remember that they were slowly weaning me off of all the drugs I was being fed. So while I was conscious...looking back, I was still pretty out of it. I remember wanting to talk...a lot! People joked that I had been asleep for two months so I was making up for lost time. I was just so excited and happy to be alive! I had ideas and plans, and I wanted to share them with everyone! I remember the doctors and nurses being amazed that I was talking aloud even with the trach in my throat. One nurse said, "In 30 years of nursing, I have never seen anyone talk with that size trach in their throat."

I woke from my coma around March 15th and actually went home on April 1st. Friends and family who had visited wanted to come back and see me now that I was actually conscious and alive. My days were filled with occupational therapists, physical therapists, doctors, nurses, nutritionists, etc. I lived for visiting hours when I could see my wife and family and friends. Because of the fear of infection, everyone coming in my room had to put on disposable scrubs over their clothes, gloves, and even a mask. I'll never forget the feeling of kissing my wife through that blue gauze mask for the first time after waking up. It was nearly better than the first time we had ever kissed at all. Well, maybe not that good but.... I know I cried then because I'm crying now just writing about it. I was so thankful that she was there. She felt so good, and she smelled so good. I felt like we had been apart forever.

As people would come to visit, they would put the scrubs, gloves, and masks on right outside my room. So I could see who was there to visit, but I had to wait for them to get dressed before they could come in. I'll never forget lying in bed just watching the clock waiting for visiting hours to begin. I would get so excited as my family and friends came to visit. The one visitor who never got to come in was my baby girl Hannah. She was only six years old at the time, and so she wasn't old enough to visit. We didn't want her to see me like that anyway. I wasn't a very pretty sight. Bandages everywhere looking like a half wrapped mummy....hooked up to all kinds of machines and wires... Daddy was coming home soon enough, but it was hard. So hard to be away from her.

Chapter 7 – Therapy (or Torture!)

The two weeks I spent actually awake in the hospital were all about getting me well enough to go home. Each day I would spend what seemed like hours with both physical and occupational therapists. At first they were working with just getting me to be able to sit upright in the bed. Then to move my arms. Then to squeeze my hands. I could not even begin to close my left hand, and that definitely scared me. To this day, no one has been able to explain why my left hand was so messed up except that it was burned worse than the right one. To me, that didn't explain why I couldn't bend my fingers? To this day, I still can't completely close my left hand into a fist. Even after many many hours of PAINFUL physical therapy, I can only close it about 75% maybe. (On a side note, one of my concerns was being able to grip a golf club again. My son, being the eternal optimist, pointed out to me that loosening my grip could only help my golf swing! Thanks, Luke. I love you too.) I still had so many wires coming in and out of my body that moving anything required quite a bit of careful maneuvering around.

Probably the scariest day of therapy was the first day they decided to get me up and have me sit in a chair. Now remember, I had been in a coma for two months. Think about how crazy that would be just for a minute? Two months of your life for which you have no memory at all. For people who have never been through it, it's hard to explain that I had to have help just sitting up in bed. Then I had to have help swinging my legs over the side of the bed. Then Dennis, my drill instructor/therapist, asked me if I could stand up. In the few days Dennis had been torturing me with his sadistic version of physical therapy, we had quickly developed a love/hate relationship. Mostly hate on my part. Even though in my mind I wanted to do twice as much therapy as was required so I could get back to my normal life, actually enduring it was another thing entirely. EVERYTHING was so hard. Hard to move, hard to sit, hard to reach for my cup of water, hard to eat...it was almost like being an infant again. And it would get worse. Back to Sgt. Dennis's question asking me if I could stand up. I thought that was about the dumbest thing anyone had ever asked me. I'm a grown man. Of course, I can stand up...And then came probably the scariest and most humbling experience of my entire ordeal. After they helped swing my legs to the side of the hospital bed, I placed both feet on the floor and tried to stand. When I say that nothing happened, even that may be an overstatement. I pushed up on my feet and nothing moved! I couldn't stand! Not even a little bit! NOW I was freaked out. Why wouldn't my legs move? Were they burned so badly that I couldn't even stand? And if I couldn't stand, I damn sure wouldn't be able to walk. For some reason, I didn't get emotionally upset though. I didn't cry. I just looked at Dennis and said, "What the heck, dude?" I think I remember him snickering sarcastically and saying, "What's wrong, Jim? I thought you could stand." So he tortured me AND he has jokes. Great! One of their first goals was to get me over to the chair (only a couple of feet from my bed) and have me sit up for 45 minutes or so. Looking back, that seems easy, but it most definitely was not. Not to mention they saved the worst bit of torture for after I was finally situated in the chair. I have no memory of what it's called, but Dennis and another female therapist explained that I had to wear this contraption in my mouth for about an hour each day. Its intended purpose, they said, was to stretch my mouth so that I would be able to eat normally after healing. I didn't understand that my neck and face had been burned pretty badly and that as the skin healed, it would tighten around my mouth.

This oral torture device had to be pried into my mouth with two hands. It left me sitting there looking much like Hannibal Lecter in my mind. As other visitors would walk by my room during visitors' hours in ICU, I guarantee you that as they got a glimpse of me they thought that this thing was put in my mouth to stop me from biting people! And it hurt so badly! But...Dennis told me that if I ever wanted to be able to take a bite out of a thick, juicy cheeseburger again, I'd better do what he said to do. So I did.

Looking back, the two weeks spent in the hospital after waking up from my coma were a blur. Visits from family and friends, phone calls from old friends, therapy, therapy, and more therapy.

Let me share with you a few more memories that stand out from that time in the hospital before we move on to the real reasons I want to write this book. My wife tells the story of one of the first times she got to see me on the night of my accident after arriving at the hospital. My mother was with her, and I apparently was all bandaged up and my head was extremely swollen. At this point, none of them knew how badly I'd actually been burned. My wife raised up the sheet at the foot of my bed and peered underneath. My mother said to her, "What are you doing?" Joanna said, "I'm making sure his hoo-ha is okay!" My mother replied, "I don't care about his hoo-ha!" My wife shot back, "Well, sorry but I sure do!" I've told that story many times, and I still laugh out loud picturing the two of them together at the foot of my bed having that awkward conversation.

Normally, I'm a pretty shy and private person. However, all of the meds they had me on definitely lowered my inhibitions. One of the crazier embarrassing comments I made to a nurse was, as she was changing my hospital gown, I made sure to point out to her that "I'm a grower, not a shower!"

Anyone who knows me knows I would die a thousand deaths before making that comment to anyone much less a complete stranger!

Also, a word of advice. Obviously, while in a coma for two months, a urinary catheter and rectal catheter had to be inserted to get rid of waste. If you can ever avoid having a rectal catheter or foley or whatever the heck they call it, AVOID IT AT ALL COSTS! Pulling that thing out of you in the middle of the night and not bothering to tell you that it has an inflated football at the end of it is NOT FUN NOR PAINLESS! Oh. My. God. Enough said.

Finally, one day Cigna (our insurance company at the time) decided I was ready to go home. The hospital staff wanted to keep me there to do my therapy, but Cigna decided I could do it at home. No doubt, a major factor in their decision was that they had already nearly paid out my $2 million lifetime limit in claims. Yes...$2 million! How insane is that? In two months, my insurance company paid out nearly $2 million to my health care providers. Don't get me wrong. I am so very thankful for everything that everyone did for me. Doctors, nurses, therapists, etc...But $2 million?

Chapter 8 I Remember

I have so many memories of my hospital stay. I remember my mother sitting at the foot of my hospital bed telling me what an incredibly strong and brave woman my wife Joanna was. How she was just handling everything without missing a beat. None of that surprised me. I knew what an incredible woman she was and still is.

I remember everyone telling me that I had to get back to Fitzgerald and that I was going to be amazed at how the entire town had rallied around me and my family. How there were purple and gold "Praying for Puckett" signs in yards and business windows all across my hometown! That was very humbling to me.

I remember my brother beside my bed, rubbing the top of my head, telling me how much he loved me and that I was his hero. I remember him telling me about all of my former students and players who were calling to check on me.

I remember seeing my wife for the first time after waking up. I remember thinking that she was the most beautiful sight I had ever seen, and I just wanted to kiss her lips so badly. And I did! Right through her surgical mask!

I remember the first time I talked to my son Luke on the phone after waking up. He was adamant that he was sleeping in the room with me when he got back to Augusta, and no one was going to stop him. I missed him so much!

I remember being so very thirsty all of the time, and all I wanted to drink was green G2 Gatorade. The incredible nurses at the Burn Center ICU got me an entire case and kept my cup full at all times.

I remember my best friends from Covington – Misto, Helmsie, and Peek Daddy – walking into see me one day. I was so happy to see them I just started crying. Just like Trace Adkins says in his song, you definitely find out who your friends are when something like this happens. Stu Baby, Hank, and Paul McSwain are a few others who either called or showed up – offering their help or whatever they could do for me and my family. There are many, many others. Names aren't necessary. They know who they are.

I remember the night a big black man walked into my room at about 3:00 AM with two young girls who were nursing students. He sat in a chair at the edge of my bed while these students began taking what seemed like a million staples out of me. I won't say it was painless, but it wasn't too bad because of the meds. I just felt like a guinea pig. Strange.

I remember the day they transferred me out of ICU to a regular room, and I passed by the Burn Unit ICU where families of other burn victims were gathered. They lined the hallway and clapped loudly for me in unison as I was wheeled by. They were so happy that I had made it, and I guess it gave them hope that maybe their loved ones would make it too. Tears of happiness and joy streamed down my face as I enjoyed their applause. I had made it!

I remember all of the pictures and signs on my hospital room wall. Pictures of family, friends, students, and teachers. I remember a conversation I was having with a nurse when I made the comment, "I am so thankful for you and the other nurses. I honestly don't know how you do what you do day after day after day." She looked at me and smiled before replying, "No, Mr. Puckett, I don't know how YOU do what you do. Dealing with 750 kids all day long 5 days a week. So, thank you!" It was then that I realized that God gives us all different gifts, abilities, and tolerances. Dealing with blood and needles and God knows what else was nothing for this ICU nurse, but the thought of overseeing a school with 750 third, fourth, and fifth graders terrified her. Go figure.

I remember the day they sent us home. We were terrified! Joanna was going to have to be a 24 hour triage nurse in addition to a wife and mother. We were scared to death yet excited to finally get out of the hospital. I still could barely walk, even with a walker. And so begins the rest of our story.

Chapter 9

Your Daddy's Coming Home Today

My daughter Hannah was in the first grade at J.S. Pate Elementary School in

Cordele, GA when my accident happened. As I mentioned before, my wife was bound and determined to keep Hannah's life as normal and uninterrupted as possible during this crisis. Other family members suggested that maybe Hannah should live with my brother Wayne and his family in Thomaston, GA and go to school there until I recovered. Joanna politely thanked them for the offer but said no. She would handle it. And handle it she did. Our neighbors across the street from our home were Keith and Robin Carter. They have two children, Somer and Logan. Logan was probably 12 at the time, and Somer was in kindergarten. Somer and Hannah were best friends. I make fun of Robin all the time because she's one of those crazy animal lovers who will take in any stray animal who shows up at her doorstep; this time she took our daughter in when we needed her most. We can never repay Robin and her family for helping us. They volunteered to keep Hannah for Joanna from Monday through

Thursday so she could be at the hospital with me. Joanna's Aunt Lynn Wessinger spent two entire weeks at our home watching Hannah, and her best friend Stacey Bell also spent an entire week at our home watching Hannah during the first several weeks of our ordeal. Where would we have been without these people? I thank God every day for putting these angels in our lives. Joanna's brother Vic Weaver, sis-in-law Beverly Weaver, and brother Mark Weaver all visited with Jo in Augusta and made sure she had whatever she needed. Our niece Courtney and fiancé Scott Alverson spent several nights with Jo in Augusta. She just mainly needed her family to be there...and they were. Even my mother-in-law Weezie came to visit me! The Ol' Battle Ax! She actually loved it when I called her that! Some of our other angels included Joi Kinnett, Vicki Futch, Katrina Vaughn, and Morgan Wiggins. All teachers from my elementary school who took it upon themselves to make sure that Joanna was okay all the time. There were so many more. Who was the biggest trooper of all? That would be our daughter – the incomparable Hannah Christine Puckett. How many six year olds do you know of who could have dealt with that situation? She never wavered or showed any sign of stress. She kept her studies up and allowed her Mom to be with me without worrying to death if she was okay. I can't even begin to describe her strength throughout all of this. It amazes me to this day. She never cried at night on the phone or whined for Joanna to come home. It was just, "You take care of Daddy. I'll be fine." What?!! Who does that at six years old?

Joanna said Hannah broke down only one time that she remembers. All of the students and staff at my school had made a DVD for me of different students and teachers wishing me well. The soundtrack to the DVD was Darius Rucker's "Alright". As Joanna was driving them to the movie theater one weekend, she showed the DVD to Hannah in the car. All of a sudden, Hannah burst into tears and began sobbing hysterically. Jo quickly pulled the car over, got in the back seat, and just held her and told her it was all going to be okay. To this day, Hannah gets a little upset each time that song plays on the radio.

For some reason, Hannah made it known to her mother that her Daddy was going to come home from the hospital on April 1st. We don't know where she got that date, and she doesn't either. Remember she was just six years old at the time. Guess what day I got released from the hospital? April 1st! How crazy is that? Hannah will always remember that day because the school secretary came over the loudspeaker in her classroom and said, "Hannah Puckett? Your Daddy's coming home today!" Of course, she lost it and cried and cried, but this time they were happy tears!

There are so many crazy things that happened once I was released. I will only bore you with a couple of stories from our four hour car ride home. After spending the first night in the apartment the hospital had furnished for my wife, we began our pilgrimage back home to Cordele. I'm still amazed that I was able to climb the steps to and from that second story apartment. Amazed even more that I didn't fall and careen to my death. Jo literally had to help me take every step. It was awful, but like everything else, we got it done.

As we left the next morning, we decided to stop at Waffle House for breakfast. Now remember that I could barely walk or even stand on my own. Getting out of our 2003 Honda Pilot was somewhat easy because it was high off the ground. It was much easier getting down from a higher seat than getting up. After we finished the best meal I'd had in nearly three months, we were ready to leave. I slowly slid my legs sideways from under the booth. Joanna had my walker in front of me as I braced one hand on the table, the other on my walker and tried to stand. Also remember that I'm 6'4' so those booths are a little low to me. I couldn't stand. I pushed up with my feet as hard as I could, but I could not move. So now I start sweating profusely because I'm embarrassed in front of all the other customers. I didn't know what to do. Jo didn't know what to do. This was all new to us. We hadn't quite thought it through when we decided to eat breakfast here. Finally, with her help and my determination not to ask any Waffle House patrons if they would mind carrying me out to my car, I slowly began to stand. I got about halfway up and couldn't go any further. I know that sounds crazy, but I literally could not stand all the way up. So now I was really in a dilemma. I was either going to fall back in the booth or crash land in the Waffle House floor...neither one of which was very appealing to me. Both were going to hurt, and some of my brand new skin was definitely going to break and blood was going to spill. My wife seems to have a lot of problems with her lower back these days. I promise you that it all probably stems from her trying to keep me from falling in the Waffle House floor in Augusta, GA that day. The time that I was half standing, half sitting and pushing with all my might and her pulling with all her might...the time where I was looking about trying to find the softest place to land...seemed like an absolute eternity. I'm sure, however, that it was maybe 3-4 seconds. Finally, by the grace of God and my Wonder Woman wife, we managed to get me upright. Euphoria is what I felt! Along with the quickly subsiding fear of having to listen for the rest of my life as she told the story of the time I fell in the floor at the Waffle House.

We made it back to the Pilot and continued our journey home.

Now, the rest of our trip was pretty uneventful except for one thing. You know how sometimes Waffle House food hits you pretty hard and you have to find a bathroom pretty quickly? Well, imagine being in a coma for two months being fed through a tube and then stupidly deciding that one of your first meals upon leaving the hospital was going to be at Waffle House. Again, something we just may not have thought all the way through. Don't get me wrong! I love me some Waffle House, but most of my trips there were usually after long nights of partying and drinking in college and in my younger years. So...we're driving along and my stomach begins to talk to me. If you've ever driven from Augusta, GA to anywhere else in Georgia actually, there's no easy way to get there. It's a lonely highway with only a few establishments at least until you get to Macon. You all know that feeling of having to go to the bathroom and you know there's no bathroom for miles and miles. It has to rank up there with one of the worst feelings of all time – period. So, worst case scenario you may have to stop and run in the woods, right? Wrong! I could barely stand or walk. Not to mention the $2 million dollars of new skin I was wearing so running into the woods was definitely not an option. I don't remember how long this panic went on before we finally saw a BP station come into view. Nothing else around...just this BP station with an old guy selling fresh boiled peanuts from a stand out front. I felt like I'd discovered gold I was so happy! Another crisis averted! Or so I thought.

So we pull up to the side of the little store where the bathrooms were located. Jo goes in to get the key. I could barely sit so I had one of those portable raised donut holes that fit over a toilet seat. My stomach was about to violently explode, and I still had to get from the back seat of our SUV into the bathroom. Jo helped me stand up and slowly but quickly walk to the restroom. She handed me my donut hole. (This is horrible!) She said, "Do you want me to come in with you?" Now, first you must know that we're one of those couples who keep things like using the bathroom PRIVATE. We have never, ever, in nearly twenty years together used the bathroom in front of each other. So when she asked if I wanted her to come in and witness what was going to probably be the most violent and possibly even fatal bowel movement I had ever had, my answer was an emphatic, "OH MY GOD, NO! GET OUT NOW!" To this day, I think she was just offering to be nice and fulfill her wifely duties. I promise you there was a HUGE look of relief on her face when I told her no! So she leaves and I somehow get the donut down on the toilet and fall on top of it. I kid you not. If you've ever seen the bathroom scene in Dumb and Dumber, this rivals it. I am in no way exaggerating even a little bit. It was absolutely horrible. I had seen the term violent diarrhea before, but never understood. Now I understand. I couldn't stop. It went on and on and on. And then, to my horror, I began to see shadows standing outside the door. I heard voices. A small line of people had gathered waiting to use the men's room that I was currently destroying. I hear my wife explaining to them that I had just gotten out of the hospital and it may be a while. Please go away! Please go away! Oh God, please go away! Of course they didn't go away. Just stood in line waiting for me to exit the crime scene. I began to sweat profusely. I honestly don't know what was worse. The pain I felt while trying to find a bathroom or the total embarrassment I was about to feel when I had to walk out in front of these strangers. Not to mention that I could NOT walk and would have to be helped out of the bathroom by my wife! While carrying a horribly smelly toilet ring in a garbage bag! I somehow managed, with Joanna's help, to get out and walk past everyone in line and get back in the car.

Definitely one of the most embarrassing moments of my life. I pity the next person who walked in that BP bathroom. It's funny now, and we always laugh when we drive by that station on the way to Augusta. We joke that there is probably a sign with my picture on it behind the desk that reads "WARNING: Do NOT give this man the key to the restroom!"

So we continued home, and I began to get very excited about seeing my baby girl Hannah. I had not seen her since the day of my accident on January 16th. Today was April 1st. When we finally made it to Cordele after nearly four hours in the car, we drove to the ballpark where Hannah was with our neighbors the Carters. I was in the backseat. Jo got out and told Hannah that Daddy was finally home. She came running up to the side door of the car. As my wife opened the door, I expected Hannah to see me and jump up in my arms and have this wonderful movie moment reunion. But we both forgot that

Daddy looked extremely different than the last time Hannah had seen me. I was MUCH skinnier, had no facial hair, very little hair on my head which for some reason was growing back shockingly blonde, and various body parts were still wrapped up in lots of white gauze and bandages. Not to mention my face and neck looked like I had a severe sunburn. When Hannah saw me, she did a double take and stopped in her tracks! Her face told me that she was very confused. That was supposed to be her Daddy but it didn't look like her Daddy. I said, "It's okay, baby. It's Daddy. Come see me!" She still was very unsure and looked like she was about to cry. Her mama assured her that I was indeed her Daddy. I couldn't tell if she was so upset because she really wasn't sure if it was me or if she was just worried that I obviously had been hurt really badly if I looked like this? We finally convinced her that I was really me, and she climbed in the car. I just wanted to grab her and hold her to me and never let her go, but I didn't want to freak her out any more than she already was. So our first hug wasn't exactly what I'd imagined, but it was still so awesome and wonderful. I was so glad to be alive and back home with my family!

The next several weeks were just more of a blur. I was still taking pain meds so my memory of it all is a bit foggy. I remember friends and family coming to visit and bringing meals for us. I remember the banner hanging at my house signed by all my teachers and students. Thank you, Joi Kinnett! I remember physical and occupational therapists visiting and torturing me. I still couldn't stand up from the couch on my own, even after being able to walk with a walker. That walker got on my nerves and only lasted a day or two.

Poor Jo was such an amazing trooper through all of this. She had to bathe me, clean and wrap wounds, wait on me nearly hand and foot 24/7. I was pathetic, but she never once complained (not to me anyway!). She just took care of me and Hannah and whatever else needed to be done. I remember eating McDonald's Chicken Nuggets, popsicles, and green G2 Gatorade. Those three things were about all I wanted for weeks.

One of the funniest moments that happened during that time was what we call the bloody shower scene. You have to understand that most of my body was covered with new skin. It was as soft as a newborn baby's skin and very likely to break and bleed at any given moment. If it got too dry, it cracked and bled. If I rubbed up against something, it bled. So...my left foot was severely burned. So bad that my wife said the doctors actually considered amputating it. Thank God I wasn't involved in that conversation because it would have been ugly. Thankfully they chose to save the foot, but it was definitely the most burned and scarred up part of my body. We had to constantly clean it and bandage it. During one of these clean and re-bandage sessions, the back of my left foot where your Achilles tendon is located literally sprung a leak. A fishing line sized streak of blood shot from my foot each time I arched my foot a certain way. And when I say shot I mean shot across the room. Then I could arch my foot back to normal and it stopped. Joanna completely freaked out! As I could now walk again, we wrapped it in a wash cloth, and I hobbled quickly to the shower. For some reason, this struck me as hilarious, and I couldn't stop laughing. I was laughing so hard! Once in the shower, I began to play around. I'd arch my foot and watch as a tiny line of blood shot out like Spiderman shooting a web. Then I'd close it. Then I'd arch my foot again and shoot something else with my bloody web! It was crazy! Joanna was not laughing. She was worried that I was going to bleed to death and was begging me to let her call an ambulance. I could barely answer her because I was laughing so hard. The more I laughed, the madder she got. I finally caught my breath and assured her that I wasn't going to bleed to death with the tiny thread of blood shooting out of my foot. After she begged me to stop playing and get out of the shower, we got my foot all bandaged up and stopped the bleeding. We found that many times you just have to laugh at yourself to deal with everything, or you'll go nuts. Yet another lesson learned.

Chapter 10 – What Next?

So I'm finally getting better and very slowly getting back to being me. I could walk and even stand up from the couch on my own. That seems so trivial now, but it was horrible that I had to get my wife or son to literally grab my hands and pull me into standing position whenever I had to leave the sofa.

Remember how I said how excited I was when I woke up from my coma? I can't explain it, but as I said, I knew then what I wanted to do with the rest of my life. I wanted to write books and become a motivational speaker. I just knew I had an awesome story to tell, and that my story could help and encourage other people. I was so ready to get started.

Chapter 11 – Understanding (or not) God's Plan

Over the next few years, many things happened to get where I am today. I'll tell you about them in not much detail because

I'm dying to get to the real reasons for writing this book.

As I told you earlier, at the time of my accident, I was in my second year as an assistant principal at Ben Hill Elementary School. Getting back to my students and teachers was so very important to me. Going back to work was tough. Against everyone's wishes, I went back to work part time on May 1, 2010. One month after leaving the hospital. I thought I was ready, but looking back now I had absolutely no business going back to work. My principal at the time was a somewhat strange lady. She is one of those people who acts like she's the Christian of the year, but in reality....mmmm...not so much. I have never and will never profess to be a perfect person in any way. I wasn't a perfect assistant principal, but I worked my tail off. Anyone (teachers, students, support staff, etc.) who worked with me will tell you I always did everything I could for teachers and students alike. Teaching is a hard profession. Teachers need administrators who have their backs. I like to think that's the kind of administrator I was. I tried to be professional at all times; I tried to have fun with teachers and students; and I always tried to go above and beyond the call of duty.

My principal never once asked me how I was doing after I came back to work. She never once stopped by my office to check on me or see if I needed a break. In fact, she seemed somewhat put off by all the attention I was receiving because of my accident. I thought that a bit strange, but I try my best not to judge other people. I just went about doing my job as best as I could. I finished the last month of school and looked forward to recuperating at home over the summer so I could be at full strength when school started again.

I won't go into great detail, but I thought the next school year was very successful. I was getting stronger all the time and finally beginning to feel like my old self. I took care of my teachers, took care of my students, and looked forward to moving into our brand new school building the following year.

The last couple of weeks of that school year – my first full year back after my accident – changed my life. My superintendent walked in my office one day and said she needed to speak to me. She told me that my principal had told her that my job was not getting done. I nearly fell backward out of my desk chair. I had no idea what she had been about to say, but those were the last words I'd expected to hear. My job not getting done? Are you kidding me? My job was getting done and then some. I was beginning to realize what was happening, and it took all I had to remain calm and professional. My principal had given me my end of year evaluation the previous week. My evaluation was satisfactory but she had marked a couple of things on the form that I blatantly disagreed with. As is my right, I responded in writing to her remarks. I was extremely professional and was very careful with my words, but I wasn't going to let her make statements on my evaluation which I and everyone else in the building knew to be untrue without at least clarifying my feelings. That should have been the end of it. Please also understand that I worked with some absolutely fantastic educators. People who would do anything to help their students, fellow teachers, and me. My principal was jealous of my relationship with our teachers and staff. She will deny this vehemently, but not a teacher at our school will tell you otherwise. People in our small south Georgia community apparently were making their thoughts known that they felt I should be the principal when we headed into our new building. I never acknowledged nor encouraged such talk. If anyone ever asked me about it, I simply said that I was the assistant principal, and I support my principal in whatever she needs me to do – period. I had plenty of reason and opportunity to bash her actions, but not once did I ever do that publicly. It wasn't my place. I won't go into my thoughts and observations of her because it's not important, and it's not what this book is about. But... her actions have made me very leery of trusting those in positions of power or anyone for that matter. My superintendent asked me to tell her everything about my relationship with my principal as well as my thoughts about her. I did just that. I explained that most teachers and parents and staff members came to me if they had a problem or request. I explained that they did so because they were afraid of getting their heads chopped off by the principal. It was a well-known fact that the only way to get her to do something new in our building was to make it seem as if it was her idea in the first place. Teachers and staff members were afraid of her – period. I never bashed her to other staff members. No matter how much I disagreed with her actions, I supported her because I was her assistant principal and she was my boss. I was very professional in my talk with the superintendent, but I was honest. Looking back, maybe honesty is not what she was looking for. On the last day of post-planning before everyone headed home for the summer, our superintendent came to tell me that I was to be transferred to the middle school for the next school year and would assume the position of academic coach – not an assistant principal. She then gathered the staff to tell them the news. Our principal wanted the superintendent to deliver the news of my transfer because she knew it was going to come as a shock, and she knew that they were NOT going to like it. Our superintendent told the staff that it was her decision to move me to the middle school – not the principal's. As I mentioned before, the teachers and support staff at that school were excellent. They were smart, caring, and definitely not naïve. So they all knew what was going on from the minute they heard it announced. I stayed in my office during the announcement because I just couldn't bear it. I was beyond upset. I had rushed a nearly fatal accident recovery to hurry up and get back to my teachers and students because I loved my job so much. I loved THEM. Now someone, out of jealousy and ignorance, was taking that away from me. I had never been so hurt or angry in my life.

After the announcement in the school cafeteria of my "transfer", teachers began filing into my office, looks of shock and dismay on their faces. Some were crying; some were just extremely pissed off. I was both – trying not to let the tears come out in front of my colleagues. It was one of the worst days of my life. I don't remember much more of that day. I just remember driving home in a fog, feeling so lost and not understanding at all. I vaguely remember telling my wife about all of it. She is extremely protective of me and was ready to decapitate someone. She knew how hard I worked to get back to work and how much I loved my teachers and students. We talked about it, fussed about it, and then prayed together about it. I asked God what to do. I asked him to lead me where he wanted me to be and have me do what he wanted me to do. If that meant going to the middle school as the academic coach, that's what I would do. I didn't understand, but I learned long ago that it's not my place to understand God's plan – just to follow it. Another lesson learned.

(*Since this book was initially published, my then principal actually came to me and apologized for her actions. In February of 2016, nearly five years after losing my job as her assistant principal, she apologized to me. I accepted her apology. She actually said the words "I'm sorry" about five times during our conversation, and I honestly believe it to be heartfelt and sincere. Hopefully, we'll talk more later, but those words meant a lot to me.)

That was a hard summer. As an educator, I had always looked forward to the new school year after summer break. It has a sense of renewal, of everything being new again. All the classrooms are bright and clean. The floors are buffed to a shine. It's always my favorite time of the school year. But this was different…I was going to a new school. A school I didn't choose. And no matter how the superintendent tried to classify this as a "transfer", it was first and foremost a demotion. And everyone in my small town knew it. A demotion which took away my pride as well as about $7000 per year out of my pocket.

Fitzgerald, GA is a small town of about 22,000 people in southwest Georgia. One of those towns where everyone knows everyone's business – or at least most of them think they do. So many of the teachers at my new school had heard of my transfer. What did they think? What exactly did they hear? Will they accept me? These were just a few of the questions I had as I walked into Ben Hill Middle School for the first time that following fall. I met with the superintendent again, and I met with my new principal. I assured them both that I had decided to just close my mouth and go to work because that's what I do. I also assured the superintendent that she had made a mistake in believing that my job at the elementary school was not being done. I set out to prove to her and everyone else that I was going to succeed in whatever position I was in.

I set out to become the best academic coach I could be – with plans of getting back to being an administrator as quickly as I could. Our principal and assistant principal, were both fantastic to me. I like to think that they both realized pretty quickly that I was a positive addition to the Ben Hill Middle School staff. One afternoon, sitting in my office as the day was coming to a close, the principal said something to me that still to this day means more to me than she'll ever know. She said "Jim, you know the superintendent and I are close friends. We talk a lot in the afternoons and evenings on the phone just friend to friend." I just said, "Yes ma'am?" She went on, "I just want you to know that after seeing all you've accomplished and the work ethic and positive attitude you've brought here to the middle school, I told her that she made a big mistake about you. She got duped, and I told her exactly that." I wanted to shout "Hell yes!" and give a big Tiger Woods fist pump, but somehow I refrained. I think I just said thank you very much and went on about my business. I just felt validated. I hoped upon hope that our esteemed superintendent would see fit to at some point apologize to me, to tell me she was wrong about me. She never did that. Not even close.

After that year, our principal took a job at the board office. She told me herself that she, in her exit interview, recommended that they hire her current assistant principal as the principal and hire me as the assistant principal. I was elated. Finally, I had done the right thing by coming to the middle school and just going back to work. Once again, my job performance was going to get me where I wanted to go. Except it didn't…The BOE did hire our assistant principal as the new principal. When I interviewed with him to be the new assistant principal, a position he had already told me would be mine, he asked me to do something different. He explained that a black female had applied and her curriculum experience was off the charts. She was going to be great for us. He asked me to move into the graduation coach position and also become the athletic director. He then told me, "I have two years left until I retire, and I want you to be ready to step into my seat as principal at that time." What can I say? I trusted the man. He was a no nonsense, no politics kind of guy – much like me. So that's what I did.

The first female assistant principal he hired, the one who was supposed to be so great for us, turned out to have a few screws loose in her head. Without going into detail, she was gone not long after Christmas break. Instead of hiring a new assistant principal, we finished out the year without one. Which is to say many of those duties fell to me. Which I didn't mind because I felt I was learning for the future. So that summer when they interviewed for the AP job, I didn't even receive an interview. It didn't bother me all that much because I felt our two year plan for me to become principal was still in place.

To make a long part of this shorter, suffice it to say that at the end of my second year as graduation coach and athletic director, despite a proven and successful track record, I was still not hired as the principal. Not only that, but since my position was funded with federal funds that ran out that year, I also didn't have a position at all. After seventeen years in education, I was out of a job. I hadn't looked for another job during the school year because I trusted what my principal had told me – that he was going to have me in his position when he retires. But he didn't make that happen. I'm not sure how hard he tried, but the superintendent (yes, the same one) made it quite clear in my interview for the principal's position that no matter what the principal had told me, it was not solely his decision. They hired his assistant principal as the new principal. My interview had gone as well as it could have gone. I was proud of everything I said in that interview. Do I think I was the best person to be the new leader of Ben Hill Middle School? I most certainly do. But I've learned that the best person for the job doesn't always get hired. I guess, even at 47 years of age, I'm still quite naïve about a lot of things. It's just so hard for me to think that people may have hidden agendas in the things they do or the decisions they make. Again, I'm not perfect in any way, but I like to think I'm a straight shooter. Someone who'll look you in the eye and be honest with you. That's who I try to be each day.

So...I'm out of a job after seventeen years as a teacher, coach, and administrator. Out of a job in my hometown! A town I came back to work in for what I had planned to be the rest of my career. Remember I hadn't looked for a job because I trusted what my principal had told me about sitting in his chair after two years. And now not only was I definitely not in his chair, but I had no position at all. I won't even go into all that I did at Ben Hill Middle School, but I will tell you that no one and I mean no one there worked any harder than I did. Once again, many teachers were upset at my dismissal but what could they do? We had several who may have worked just as hard, but no one worked any harder for the students and teachers than I did. That's not being boastful at all. It's the simple truth.

So now what? What choices do I have? I have a wife, a daughter in 5th grade, and a son in college to provide for? What am I going to do now? For several years now, I had been involved in a lawsuit against the manufacturer of the gas can that blew up on me. After leading me to believe we would settle for at least $7 million and after turning down their first offer of $1.1 million, a judge eventually granted a summary judgement to the defendant. More on this later, but the bottom line is I get zero, zilch, nada... So that money that we had been promised was coming did not come. I immediately filed for unemployment – something I never thought I'd have to do. I think I received $323 per week for sixteen weeks. A definite help. I could have requested a hearing regarding the elimination of my position but it was pointless. They had crossed all their t's and dotted all their i's. The thought of having to legally make someone give me a job sickens me anyway. I don't want to work for a system who doesn't seem to value what I do.

But I still have to provide for my family. I applied for several assistant principal's positions in surrounding counties, but all had pretty much been filled by that point. I ended up with really only one option. I would have to cash out my teacher retirement fund and live on that for the next year while we planned on what to do next. Talk about scary! I've invested seventeen years into my career, and now I have no choice but to pull my money out to survive. Retirement nest egg is gone. I filled out the necessary paperwork, and soon received a little over $45,000 after taxes. Enough for us to survive for the next year, but not what I wanted to do.

Someone also mentioned to me that I could apply for government assistance with buying food. Food stamps! EBT. My first thought was no way am I going to apply for food stamps. In my mind, only lazy people who didn't want to work were on food stamps. But as I read more about the program and actually applied and had a phone interview, the lady explained to me that cases like mine were exactly what this government program was for. I reluctantly agreed and began receiving $612 per month to buy food for my family. We often purchased groceries out of town because we didn't want anyone to see us use our EBT card. Silly perhaps, but it made me feel as though I had failed as a man.

We also decided to move back to Fitzgerald, GA. We were immediately glad to be back in my hometown. My daughter absolutely loved it here from day one. Changing schools in the middle of a school year can be very traumatic for a middle school girl. Our daughter handled it without missing a beat. My wife and I knew she would make friends easily enough because she rarely meets a stranger, and she already knew most of the teachers there as well. But we figured she would definitely have some bad days early on as she adjusted to new things and people and missed her old friends. She never had even one bad day. Her exact words to me on her second day after I picked her up were, "Daddy, I like this school 10 times better than my old school!" To us, this was just another sign from God that we were in the right place.

We were back home around family and friends. We both felt at peace here from the very beginning. We knew that we now had to decide how we were going to provide for our family after my retirement funds ran out.

Chapter 12 – My New Career

As I told you earlier, I knew in my heart when I awoke from my coma exactly what I wanted to do. I knew that I could help people by telling my story and the things I've learned over the years. I'm pretty sure I told my wife within the first 48 hours of waking up that I wanted to write a book and become a motivational speaker. I literally could not wait to get started! Since my accident over five years ago, we've been through so much. Ups and downs and all arounds. You go to bed one night thinking your life will be one way and the next day EVERYTHING changes. Too many of us fight that change. One thing all of this has taught me is to embrace change. I fully believe that everything happens for a reason. We don't often know that reason, but we have to keep on keeping on. What choice do you have? Life is WAY too short to waste time worrying about what happened yesterday. The rest of this book is going to be me telling you about what I've learned from the various events that have happened in my life and, most importantly, what I've learned from the different people in my life. I hope you laugh, maybe cry a little, but most of all I hope you learn and are entertained. I hope when you finish with this book you feel like it was worth your while. If you do that, I've accomplished my goal.

Chapter 13 – The Lawsuit

The lawsuit is one of the reasons I've learned that you can't waste time worrying about what did or did not happen yesterday. If I did that, I would forever be depressed about the $1.1 million I turned down on the advice of my attorney because he thought there "was more money out there."

I have never sued anyone in my life. I have never even thought about suing anyone. So when my wife first told me that she had spoken with an investigator and attorney who were interested in filing a lawsuit against the company who manufactured the gas can that exploded on me, I was very skeptical. But when they came to my home and explained that there should have been a flame arrestor in the mouth of the gas can AND that the company knowingly removed the arrestor just to decrease their costs of manufacturing and thus increase their profits, I began to listen in earnest. A flame arrestor is kind of shaped like a nipple on a baby's bottle but made out of the mesh similar to a screen door. It allows liquid to be poured from the gas can, but strangely enough, prevents a flame from going back into the can. Sounds crazy but you can actually hold a lighter up to a flame arrestor and see that the flame will not go through it. I am the one who splashed gasoline on an open flame, but I NEVER thought it would ignite fumes which would then travel back through the can and explode on me. It took a while, but this attorney convinced me that this accident was NOT my fault and could have easily been prevented had the manufacturer not tried to save a few cents by taking a known safety measure out of their cans. So we filed suit against the manufacturer of the gas can. I will never forget my attorney standing in my kitchen and saying, "You know, Jim...we've settled cases like this for more than eight figures." It took only a second to deduce that he meant more than $10 million. That means that after his firm's 40% take and expenses on a hypothetical $10 million settlement, I would receive between five and six million dollars. I was dumbfounded! The most I had ever made in one year was about $60, 000 and this man was telling me I could very well end up with over $5 million! Now, let me say really quickly that no amount of money in the world can make up for what my family and I have been through with my accident. BUT I won't lie and say that money wouldn't help because it most definitely would.

I've told many people that I learned more about the law over the next few years than I ever wanted to know. Once we filed the lawsuit, we had to give depositions and statements and visit this specialist and be evaluated by that specialist and on and on and on. Our attorney told us to expect the process to take at least two years. Two years! So imagine our delight when finally the defendant's attorney asked for a mediation. There are actually firms who do nothing but mediate lawsuits between parties. I was so excited because the end seemed to be in sight. As the investigator often told us, "There's a light at the end of the tunnel...and it ain't a train!"

So we travel to Atlanta and are put up in a nice 5 star hotel. I remember joking with my wife that pretty soon, we would always be able to afford a 5 star hotel. We had dinner with our attorney at Maggiano's, had a few drinks before bed, and retired for the night dreaming about possibilities.

Neither of us had ever been to a mediation so we really didn't know what to expect when we arrived the next day. I can feel my blood pressure rising just writing about it because I know we didn't settle. And I know we should have. The mediation office was a very swanky space in downtown Atlanta. We were ushered in with our attorneys and investigator. We sat on one side of an enormous oak table, and the defendant and their attorneys sat on the other side. At the head of the table was the mediator. He explained that after his introduction and explanation of the process, the two sides would retire to separate rooms. A settlement offer would be delivered to us by the mediator. We would then either accept or counter with a higher offer. The idea being we go back and forth until an agreed upon settlement amount is reached. That's what we expected. That is definitely NOT what happened. Remember that my attorney had told me that we could possibly settle this for $10 million or more? Well, the first offer presented to us was for $300,000. The main trial attorney with us went berserk at this offer. He basically told the mediator that he could tell the defendants to go jump in a lake (but in harsher words) because they were wasting our time by offering such a low amount. He told them we were not going to sit here all day going back and forth and playing games. And we left...

We weren't overly shocked because we had been warned that the settlement most likely wouldn't get done that day. BUT...I thought we would have gotten much closer than that. Later that day, as we drove back home to South Georgia, my main attorney called. He knew I was disappointed and just wanted to reassure me that this settlement would get done. He let me know that the defendants were prepared to pay $5 million that day and that we could settle for that amount anytime I was ready. He told me that he would feel comfortable telling me to settle when the offer reached $7 million – and he was certain that it would. As I write this, I am thinking to myself, "You idiot (me – not my attorney)! Why in the world did you not say YES! Settle this NOW for $5 million!" But at the time, my attorney felt very strongly that the offer would reach $7 million.

To make a very long story somewhat shorter, a short time later we received a written offer from the defendant's attorney for a $1.1 million settlement. That meant that my 60% cut would be $660,000 minus about $205,000 in expenses for a grand total remaining of $455,000. I remember my attorney saying that he felt there was much more money out there. We really didn't even consider this offer. Several months later, as we prepared to have another mediation (requested by the defendant) at which I had already decided we were going to stay until a deal got done, everything changed. The judge in our case issued a summary judgement against us. Basically, after two years and hundreds of thousands of dollars spent by both sides, a judge was saying I could not sue for this because basically it was my fault. What?!! My attorney was dumbfounded to say the least. Defendant attorneys always file a motion for summary judgement just as a rule of thumb but very rarely is it EVER granted. Of course, in my case, it was granted. We were in shock. I won't bore you with all the details, but my attorney explained in detail why he and all the attorneys he worked with felt the judge had erred. We were going to file an appeal, and everyone seemed to feel very good about our chances. We lost that appeal. And the next appeal. And the next.

So after being told that we would settle for at least $7 million, we got nothing. Nada. Zilch. I'd be lying if I told you my wife and I hadn't already dreamed of what we do with that much money. We talked about family vacations, paying off all our bills, and all of the people we would help. We talked about changing our family's legacy forever. So yes, we were devastated. We cried. We cussed. We asked God why this happened to us. We prayed. And we prayed. And we prayed.

And then we decided that there had to be a reason God put us through this. We might not know what it was yet, but we had no choice but to keep on keeping on. We decided that God has other plans. He doesn't want us receiving so much money that we don't share our story and gifts with the rest of the world. Had we gotten a large sum of money, there is a very good chance that I would have never gone back to work and never written this book. I would have never pursued a career as an author and motivational speaker. People would not have heard my story. God has a bigger purpose for me, and I think sharing my story and life with others so they can better their own lives is that purpose.

Before I end the lawsuit chapter, let me say a couple of things about Brady Thomas, my attorney. Brady has become a great friend to me and my family over the past five years or so. I knew from day one that he was in this fight for the right reasons. Losing this lawsuit and getting me and my family nothing was probably harder on him than it was on us – honestly. I could hear it in his voice when he made the phone call to me. He was devastated. We still stay in touch on a regular basis. He's a good attorney, a good man and a good friend. Even if he did graduate from Florida State!

So, after each chapter I want to summarize the lessons I learned.

Lessons learned from the lawsuit:

1. Do not take anything for granted in life.
2. Even if you're involved in something you're very unfamiliar with, do your own homework and ask lots of questions.
3. Always do what's best for you and your family.
4. If something doesn't work out like you expected, you can't let it define the rest of your life. Keep on keeping on.
5. God doesn't always give you the answers you want. He has a plan even if you don't know what it is. Again, keep on keeping on.

Chapter 14   Surprise! Marriage is Work!

So...Joanna and I have been married for over fifteen years now. We both had been married before and were looking for more than a casual date. She loves to tell people we met at a social function, but in reality, we met one Friday night at a country bar in Griffin, GA. My brother and I were out partying with some friends, and she was there with a girlfriend from work. I remember standing in line to get in and seeing this tall redhead in a cowboy hat dancing on stage and just thought, "Damn!" She was gorgeous. We bumped into each other later that night on the dance floor, and we've literally been together ever since. We still have the napkin from that night on which she wrote her phone number for me. We like to joke that hers is the only phone number I've ever kept from a girl in the bar (true), and she tells me that I'm the only man she ever gave her real phone number (Hmmm...). Regardless, we both knew from our lengthy conversation that night that we seemed to have a lot in common. And we'd like to see each other again.

We began dating, and I was pretty much smitten from day one. Joanna lived in Conyers, GA. About an hour away from me in Thomaston. If I had the money we spent on traveling back and forth to see each other, I could give this book away for free. She was a breath of fresh air – unlike any woman I had ever met. I was 29, and she was 25. On our first official date at Longhorn's, our waitress stood by our table forever waiting for us to stop talking so she could take our order. I knew that was a good sign.

We married four years later. Our marriage is in no way perfect, but we both agree that it's apparently pretty special compared to many couples we come into contact with. We've always joked that we should hold a marriage workshop because it's apparently rocket science to some.

My son, Luke, was four years old when Joanna and I met. I let her know up front that he was the most important part of my life at that time, and she respected that. One of the dumbest things I think single parents can do is to introduce their children to every person they date. After I divorced my first wife, I dated quite a bit. My young son was confused enough by his parents split. He didn't need me to introduce him to every girl in my life. When I finally introduced Luke to Joanna, it was after we both knew this was going to be a long term relationship. She was wonderful with Luke from day one. She has always treated Luke as her own child, and that's just one of the many reasons I fell in love with her.

Even though she became Luke's stepmother, she always let me handle discipline. Not that she wouldn't correct him if needed, but any stronger discipline came from me. She didn't want to confuse him, and I think it worked well. Every family dynamic is different, and we found what worked best for us. As parents or step-parents, that's what you do. You find out what works best for your family. What may work well for Joe Blow down the street may not be what's best for you.

Luke stayed with us every other weekend and holidays and most all summers. Joanna always made sure he had his own room in our home, which she decorated usually better than any other. We wanted to make sure that he knew he was really at home when he was with us – not just visiting. We've seen families similar to ours who never let the visiting child have his or her own room in their home. How is a child going to feel comfortable in a home when he stays in the guest room each time he's there? Again, we try not to judge others, but we know what worked for us.

My wife Joanna is a free spirit to say the least. She loves to laugh and dance and live life to the fullest. She's traveled the world, jumped out of airplanes, and bungee-jumped. She will usually try absolutely anything once. She loves to try new foods, and tells me I'm just ignorant when I don't want to taste something that I tell her I don't like. Her first words are always, "Have you ever tried it?" I've learned over the years to just go ahead and try it because she will NOT let it go until I do. And to her credit (I can't believe I'm admitting this), I've actually learned to like several foods that I NEVER would have tasted otherwise. Sushi and crab legs are a few of the foods that I had never tried until Joanna "persuaded" me! Of course, now I love them both.

I am a much more introverted person. At least I used to be. It's hard to be an introvert around Joanna. She has definitely brought me out of my shell. Not that I was some shy stand in the corner guy, but I was definitely not as outgoing as she was. Many people often took my shyness as being stuck up, but I just didn't feel comfortable talking to people I didn't know well.

But you know what? We complement each other. And what do I think is the most important thing? She truly is my best friend, and deep down our family core values are the same. We both believe in strong families, trust, honesty, and integrity. We both believe children should be raised with love and discipline and should be taught respect, character, and responsibility from a very young age.

Please do not think our marriage is perfect by any means. Trust me. We argue. We disagree. We fuss. We fight. But we have rules. Rules that we always try to abide by no matter what. I'll tell you what those are at the end of this chapter.

Our friends will tell you that we are that couple who still can't keep their hands off of each other. We have always been extremely physically attracted to each other, and that attraction has only grown over the years. Our son and daughter get grossed out all the time because they catch us kissing or "making out" when they leave the room. We call Hannah our apple worm because she always tries to physically get between us when we start kissing and hugging. She's like the principal at the school dance trying to break up the couple getting a little too close.

We promised each other early on in our relationship that we would always put each other first. Our relationship comes first. I've heard too many people say, "My children come before anything and anybody!" We love our children more than the world. But we realized early on that if we didn't grow and nurture our own relationship, we probably wouldn't be together to take care of our children. So we have always made time for ourselves. From a short weekend getaway to a planned night each week where it is all about us. No children. It's really quite simple. For example, our children and all of our close friends and family know about our Friday Nights. For many years, Friday night has been our "date" night unless we have some other obligation. Most nights, it's just Joanna and I sitting on the patio in our back yard, listening to music and having a few drinks. We call it the Puckett Patio. We have a few others we sometimes invite to the Puckett Patio, but usually it's just us. It's so nice to sit together after the work week, after our daughter is asleep, and just hang out together and enjoy each other's company. It's not unusual for us to dance together under the stars barefoot in the backyard or sit in the hot tub at 2:00 AM if the mood strikes. We sing old songs, maybe kiss a little (hehe...) and just shut the rest of the world out for a few hours. We both laugh sometimes at ourselves because we still get kind of giddy each week looking forward to our Friday nights together. Joanna always puts on a pretty little sundress or something that she knows I like. I, too, try to look decent and put her favorite cologne on. It's just little things that let each other know we still care about how we look for each other. She's more beautiful today than she was the night I met her – seriously.

I think the bottom line is that a good marriage takes work. It's not rocket science, folks. You have to keep a spark in your relationship. Too many couples end up like roommates instead of husband and wife. Even when Joanna was a full-time stay at home mom, I never came home to a dirty house or her dressed in old ragged sweat pants and a dirty t-shirt. She ALWAYS fixed her hair, put on make-up, and dressed nicely for me by the time I got home. I didn't expect it, and I would have completely understood if she fudged every now and then, but she didn't. It was important to her that I knew that she wanted to look good for me. Again, I didn't expect it, but it definitely made me feel good as a man and as a husband.

I could talk forever about my wife and our relationship. She is a fantastic wife and a loving, caring mother. She is my best friend and the most passionate woman I've ever known. Her smile, her laugh, and her love for life are all infectious to all those who know her. Nothing I've said in this chapter is new. What have we learned about making our marriage work:

1. Make your relationship a priority.
2. Even when arguing, fight fair. Don't bring up the past, don't curse at each other, and stick to the subject at hand. Do not yell at each other.
3. Never go to bed mad. (That's a hard one sometimes).
4. Talk to each other about things other than your children. We talk about sports, politics, food, etc.

5. Let her know you still care about her. Not just on Mother's Day and Valentine's Day. Joanna loves yellow roses and massages so I make sure to provide those for her as often as I can. She deserves all that and more.
6. Figure out what your "Friday Night" should be. Have a night each week or at least every other week when the two of you do something you enjoy together without your children. I can't stress enough how important I think a date night should be.

Chapter 15 – Parenting

No matter what many people today would have you believe, being a parent is not rocket science either. This is another area of your life that has to be individualized to meet your specific family's needs. That's one reason I'm not a huge fan of parenting books. What works for me may not necessarily work for you. With that being said, I believe there are several constants that should be present in all parenting styles.

Joanna and I both believe that our main responsibility as parents is to raise our children to be independent productive members of society. The key word there being *independent.* So many parents today, including friends of ours, seem to do exactly the opposite. Some seem to want to keep their "babies" up under them for as long as possible. Many continue to do EVERYTHING for their children even when they're in high school and even college. Our daughter Hannah has friends in middle school who still haven't spent the night away from home. What?!! And parents who don't see anything wrong with it! Students who lose the experience of going on overnight school trips or summer camps because they won't spend the night away from home. Again, I really try (and obviously fail) not to judge, but are you kidding me? Do you actually think you're helping your children become adults by encouraging this? That is YOUR fault, Mom and/or Dad. Get mad at me or refuse blame if you want. That very first night when they go to spend the night at a friend's house and you make a big deal out of how much you'll miss them AND you then go get them when they call you at 2:00 in the morning because they're scared? You're done. Game over. That child knows he/she has you hook, line, and sinker. That's why you a – don't make a big deal out of it when they spend the night away, and b – explain that if they so choose, there will be no midnight trips to pick you up. Period.

We even have friends whose children still sleep in the bed with them! Middle school aged children! And then they don't understand why their marriage lacks intimacy. Um...you're husband sleeps in another bedroom because you allow your son or daughter to sleep with you EVERY single night of your life.

Our daughter Hannah has slept in her own room since about 16 weeks of age. I'll never forget the first night we put her down in her crib instead of the bassinet beside our bed. Joanna was SO nervous! Remember, I had been a parent for nine years so I'd been through this before. I explained to her that you can't rush in and pick her up every time you hear her cry on the baby monitor. If so, she'll realize quickly that she can get her way just by crying out. Those first few nights were not easy on my wife. She desperately wanted to go to Hannah when she cried. But by maybe the third or fourth night, the crying stopped and Hannah slept all night every night from then on. Some so called "experts" and some parents advocate waking a baby up to feed them. Again, I'm no expert, but we NEVER woke Hannah up to feed her. Trust me when I tell you they'll let you know when they're hungry. Hannah got to where she would sleep 10-12 hours straight! Joanna, especially in the beginning, would often creep quietly in her room just to make sure she was still breathing. People tell us, "Well, you were just lucky you had such a good baby." I thank God every day for my healthy children, but I don't think luck had anything to do with her sleeping through the night. We conditioned her to do it. She learned what was expected, and she went to sleep when it was time to go to sleep. Now colic, sickness, and teething are different animals all parents may sometimes have to deal with, but you get the gist of what I'm saying.

Nor have we ever had a problem with either of our children continuing to sleep in their own beds. Luke is 23, and Hannah is 12. I can count on one hand the number of times either of them has come to our bed in the middle of the night. I do remember ONCE when Hannah woke me up by tapping me on the forehead while I was asleep to tell me she had had a bad dream. I let her climb in the bed with us, and I held her while she went back to sleep. The next night she went to her bed as usual. We didn't make a big deal out of it. We watch scary movies, go to Haunted Houses, and have even taken a Ghost Tour of Savannah, GA. Our children still take their butts to their own beds at night.

I want to talk about respect. Joanna and I were taught at a very young age to respect our elders. We were both taught to always say "yes sir or no sir" and "yes ma'am or no ma'am". It's amazing how far being respectful will get you in life. I'll never forget an incident that happened when I was in elementary school – probably 2nd or 3rd grade. So the year was probably 1974 or 1975. My teacher, on the first day of school, told us that we didn't have to say yes ma'am or no ma'am to her. We could just politely say yes or no. So at the supper table that night, I explained to my parents that I no longer had to say yes sir, no sir and yes ma'am, no ma'am....I could just say yes or no. You can only imagine how that went over. My Daddy never raised his voice or even flinched. He just listened to my story and then I got the "As long as you live under my roof, you will always say yes sir, no sir and yes ma'am, no ma'am to adults. Is that understood?" "It's a sign of respect, and children should always show respect to adults." My answer? "Yes sir." Now, my Daddy was a construction worker and usually always left for work before the sun came up. But for some reason, the next morning he wanted to drive me to school. I was oblivious to his reasoning, but I soon found out when he also wanted to walk me inside the school building. As we approached my classroom door, me and my 6'3" 260 lb Daddy wearing his blue work overalls, white t-shirt, and work boots...the look on my teacher's face was probably one of great shock. I'll never forget what happened next. Daddy just politely introduced himself and asked if he could speak with her in the hallway for a moment. She agreed. I started toward my desk, but Daddy held onto my shoulder and told me he wanted me to hear this, too. His words to my teacher were soft but firm. "Ma'am," he started, "I understand how hard your job must be, and I respect how hard you work to teach my son all he needs to know. But in my house, saying yes sir, no sir and yes ma'am, no ma'am is not an option. It is required of him at home, and it is required of him anytime he is speaking to an adult. I just want to make sure we're clear on that." Ironically, she said, "Yes sir...I understand, and I apologize." My Daddy said goodbye to us both and off he went. That may have been the only time my Daddy ever drove me to school in my entire life, but it's a trip I'll never forget.

Am I telling you that you should make your children use "sir" and "ma'am" when speaking to adults? I most certainly am. This simple but oh so important life tool has been ingrained in our children since they first learned to speak. It's a habit that doesn't even cross their minds because it's so automatic. In my opinion, it's invaluable. I've always made not only my own children say it, but also my players and students. Many have told me years later how learning to say those simple words was such an asset to them later in life.

I won't go too deep into spanking, timeouts, etc. We've both spanked our children. Mostly just a pop on the butt as a toddler when needed. I know some of you are aghast right now and screaming in your head that you should never lay your hands on your child. Well, I disagree. We very rarely had to use spankings, but they were effective. Both of my children are well-adjusted, responsible, and respectful. Both will also tell you that they were very rarely spanked, but when they were – it was deserved, and it taught them a lesson. We're all entitled to our own opinions, but as a public educator, I could usually tell pretty quickly when I was dealing with children who had never been spanked. Again, I'm not saying at all that you can't raise great children without spanking them. I'm just telling you what worked for us.

You cannot enable your children. You cannot do things for them that they should be doing themselves. As a teacher, I could always tell when a student turned a project in exactly who had done the majority of the work. Luke and Hannah both know that if they had something to do for school, we would make sure they had all the necessary materials, but in no way were we going to do the work for them. If you get stuck on something, I'll help you get "unstuck", but that's it. A few weeks ago, Hannah had three school projects due in one week. She is usually awesome about getting things done early, but this time, we had a lot going on and the due dates just caught up to her. She got two of the projects done and was left with only the science project. It was Thursday night, and the project was due the next day. She had to "build" and label two organelles or cells or something like that using materials she found around the house. It wasn't that difficult but was going to take at least several hours of finding the right materials, gluing them in the shoeboxes, and labeling everything. Part of me wanted to sit down immediately and help her knock this out, but I knew I couldn't do that. It was her responsibility, not mine. After several hours of working quietly in the dining room, she called me in the room. It was already about 9:45 PM, and her bedtime was 10:00 at the very latest. She had finished with one shoebox and was about to glue everything into the next one. She asked me if I would write the labels out for the completed box and glue them to their corresponding parts. I politely asked her whose responsibility this project was. She replied that it was hers. I said, "Baby, please understand that it has nothing to do with me not wanting to help you. I know you're tired and ready to get to bed. But...this project is not my responsibility. You've known for several weeks now about this, and you've chosen to wait until the last minute to get it done. If I sit down and help you now, I'm not teaching you a thing except that I'll bail you out when something gets tough." Most twelve year olds would have begun pleading and whining at that point about how tired they were and how unfair this is. Hannah simply said, "Daddy, you're right. This is my job – not yours. You go on to bed, and I'll finish it myself. I shouldn't have waited until the last minute." I was SO proud of her! I almost sat down and helped her just for saying that! But I was strong! I told her I'd stay up with her until she finished, but I'd be in the living room reading. She went back to work and finished probably around 11:30 that night. She was sleepy and tired the next morning, but I could tell she had a sense of accomplishment that she wouldn't have had if I'd done the work for her. Another lesson learned.

I hope that none of you take anything I've said here about being a good parent personally. Joanna and I are by no means experts, but we do get told by many people that we've done a good job raising our children. Here's what I hope you take out of this chapter:

> 1. Teach your children respect from a very young age. Children should ALWAYS show respect to adults and authority figures. One easy way to do this is by teaching them to say yes sir, no sir and yes ma'am, no ma'am.

2. Raise your children to be INDEPENDENT. Start as early as possible. It is your job as a parent to make them productive members of society. If you start early, it's really easy. STOP doing everything for them. You're not helping by doing that.

3. Do NOT bail your students out of tough situations or always come to their defense. Always be there to support your children when they're right, but also be there to correct them when they're wrong.

4. Your child should not sleep in the same bed as you and your spouse on a consistent basis. It's not good for them, and it's damn sure not good for your marriage.

Chapter 16 Teaching and Coaching

I put teaching and coaching together because they are basically the same thing. A good coach is just a good teacher. I could write an entire book just on my experiences teaching and coaching. Many teachers often joke about the book they'll write one day about all of their experiences. Well, here goes mine I guess.

I totally backed into a career as an educator. After a few years as a banker and then an entrepreneur opening my own health club, I was for the first time in my life undecided about what comes next. I was 27 years old, divorced with a two year old son, and I didn't know what to do next. I had never failed at anything before in my entire life. But in the past 5 years, I had quit law school, lost a business, lost a house and truck, declared bankruptcy, and went through a divorce. I was reeling, to say the least. I then made a decision that would change my life for the better.

My younger brother Wayne had started his teaching and coaching career in Thomaston, GA at Upson-Lee Middle School. He invited me to move in with him. I took him up on it and began substitute teaching at his school.

All I can say is I fell in love with teaching. I would spend the next 17 years of my life as an educator. I taught middle school Language Arts and coached football and basketball. Later in my career, I became an administrator and athletic director. This book is to share with you what I learned from the people and experiences in my life. I learned so many lessons while teaching and coaching that I often felt I was the student.

I've always believed that you can learn something from everyone who comes into your life. It may be that you learn what NOT to do or how NOT to act, but you can still learn something.

Early on in my teaching career, I was standing in front of a group of eighth graders trying to teach them about the parts of speech. I asked the students to raise their hands to volunteer to use certain verbs I had written on the board in a sentence. A rather energetic young lady raised her hand to use the verb "were" in a sentence. I called on her and learned one of my first lessons from students. She replied, "Coach Puckett, if you were a cheeseburger, I'd eat you up!" What? I was so stunned by her bold and obviously inappropriate sentence that I couldn't speak for a few seconds. Luckily, I quickly realized that the best way to handle this was to ignore it and move on to the next volunteer. What eighth grader has the guts to say that to a teacher? I didn't know whether to laugh, get angry, or just act like it never happened. I chose the latter, and it was probably the best move. I learned that day that these eighth graders were much more brazen and confident than any back in my day. I've told that story so many times, and each time I can't help but laugh. That young lady actually went on to become a very good student and high school basketball player. The last I heard from her was when I got an invitation to her high school graduation. She then joined the military, and I'm sure she is successful in whatever she's doing.

During those initial few years of teaching, I was the eighth grade boys' basketball coach and the ninth grade football coach. I want to tell you about a student named Chester. Remember, I taught 8th grade English. Chester was an eighth grade student in my class, but he was 15 because he had failed a grade. Chester was a black male with a twin brother in the ninth grade. Chester obviously had some academic deficiencies, but he was a hard worker and one of the most polite young men I'd ever met. He and his brother lived at home with their mom, a struggling single mother who worked her tail off trying to make ends meet for her boys. Chester wore just about the same outfit to school every single day. A pair of worn jeans and an often dingy white t-shirt. I remember taking up money from teachers and buying Chester new t-shirts and a pair of jeans at Christmas. By the look on his face, you'd have thought we just gave him a new Sony Playstation. I learned a great deal from Chester, but I learned one particular lesson I'll never forget.

You see, Chester was in the eighth grade, but he was too old to play on the eighth grade football team. We allowed eighth graders who were too old to play on the middle school team the opportunity to play on the ninth grade team as long as their grades and behavior were satisfactory. Now Chester loved to play football. He was about

5'8' maybe and possibly 110 lbs soaking wet. But he gave it his all and was a pretty good athlete. He started for us in the defensive backfield and always gave 110%. I can still see his beaming smile inside his helmet after he made a tackle and came off the field. I remember that his head was so tiny we had trouble finding him a helmet that would actually fit. He was a very happy kid.

I'd never had any reason to be upset with Chester or mad at him at all. As a student, he always turned in assignments, volunteered in class, and tried his best. As a football player, he would do anything I asked on the field with only a "yes sir!". So you can imagine my disappointment when one day in the locker room after practice, Chester asked me a strange question. We had a game the next day, and Chester wanted to know if we were going to have an announcer on the P.A. system announcing the game. In high school athletics, the ninth grade team doesn't always get the same perks as the varsity team. We often had to scrounge around for referees, people to work the chains, etc. So sometimes we had an announcer, and sometimes we did not. I remember we had lost a couple of games in a row, and as coaches, we were trying to right the ship and make these boys understand the importance of playing together as a team and not just individuals. So Chester asking me if we were going to have an announcer just so (I thought) he could hear his name called out got me very upset to say the least. I'm not sure exactly what I said, but I pretty much jumped all over him. I let him know very loudly in front of other teammates and coaches that hearing his name over the loudspeaker was the very last thing he needed to worry about! That was exactly the kind of selfishness that caused us to lose the last few games! I berated him and just could not believe that this quiet, unassuming young man had actually said that. After my tirade and using Chester as an example of what we do NOT want on this team, the locker room fell silent. Chester just looked up at me and said, "Sorry, Coach." Everyone got dressed silently and went home.

It was my turn to stay behind with the players who hadn't been picked up from practice yet. As luck would have it, guess who was the very last player to be picked up that day? Yep! Chester. As he and I sat on the curb outside the locker room waiting on his mom, I was still mad and really not interested in anything he had to say. I wanted him to go home and think about what he'd said and hopefully learn from his mistake. After sitting in awkward silence for a few minutes, Chester sheepishly said, "Coach, I'm sorry for making you mad, but it's not what you think." I replied, "Really, Chester? Because what I think is you are more worried about hearing your name called out than winning a football game. That is exactly the kind of attitude we do not want around here. And from you of all people?

I'm surprised and disappointed." Chester, you're the last person I expected to worry about something that silly." Quietly but adamantly, Chester explained, "But Coach, it's not for me. It's for my Mom. You see, they charge $5 to get in our games. My mom can't always afford that so sometimes she just sits in her car in the field parking lot and listens for the announcer to call my name. She says if she can't see me play, she can at least listen for my name." My heart dropped. The oft used phrase "insert foot in mouth" does not even begin to describe what a lowlife piece of dirt I felt like at that moment. I wanted a sinkhole to open up under that school parking lot and swallow me up – never to be seen or heard from again. What a complete idiot I was! Minutes earlier, I completely called this young man out and embarrassed him in front of all his teammates because I ASSUMED he was being selfish by wanting an announcer at our football game. When all he really wanted was for his mother, who couldn't afford a ticket for the game, to be able to hear his name. Again, I don't remember my exact words, but I grabbed Chester and hugged him tight and repeated over and over how sorry I was. He just said, "It's fine, Coach. I understand." Well, it most definitely was not fine. I had made a huge mistake, and now I needed to correct it. The first thing I did, after apologizing to Chester, was to explain what happened to his mother when she arrived to pick him up. I told her what an idiot I had been, and how sorry I was. I also told her that she would NEVER have to sit in the parking lot again to "hear" her son play.

When I got home that night, I immediately called our head coach and told him what Chester had told me. He was a really good man and was just as upset about it as I was. When Chester's mom dropped him off the next day for our game, I was waiting for her in the parking lot. After Chester went inside to get dressed, I walked over to her car and she rolled down the window. I handed her a season's pass which allowed her to get into all our home games free of admission. Being the proud woman she was, she tried vehemently to refuse it. I wouldn't take no for an answer, and she eventually relented. With a tear in her eye, she simply said, "Thank you, Coach Puckett." I said, "No ma'am. Thank YOU. Because of your son, I learned a very valuable lesson yesterday. I will NEVER assume I know anything again without having all the facts." We went on to have a pretty good season, but the lesson I learned from Chester that day will always be invaluable to me.

I've always told people that in my opinion, my biggest weakness as an educator, especially early on, was that I assumed that all my students were raised similar to the way I was raised. In other words, somewhere in the middle class, parents still married and at home each night, dinners together at the table each night, someone to help them with their homework, and so on. I learned quickly, from Chester and hundreds more, that I was so very wrong. Of course, it matters where you teach, but in the schools I taught in, single parent homes were much the norm. Many students had only one parent at home, no parents at home, and some didn't even have homes. Some had a parent or both parents in jail. Some never knew from night to night where they were sleeping or if they were going to have a hot meal for dinner. Some had no place to do homework and nobody to help them do it. Many wore the same clothes several times a week – often without washing them.

You always hear people say that you can't save the world, but I think they're wrong. Anyone who's spent much time around me can tell you what my motto has always been: Just try to make your little piece of the world a better place. That's it. If we all try to do whatever it is we do for a living to the best of our ability and try to make our little piece of the world a better place, then I say we CAN change the world. I'm not just saying that to sell a book. I believe it with all my heart and soul. As a teacher and a coach, that's what I tried to do. When students walked into my classroom, I made sure they felt welcome and safe. I wanted to insure that at least for that 50 minutes of their day or whatever it was, they were going to be with someone who truly cared about them and was going to do all he could to help them learn and become a better person. I tried to be firm but fair. I tried to relate whatever I was teaching to the real world. Simply memorizing the eight parts of speech isn't going to help you get a job one day. Learning to use those parts of speech correctly when you're writing a cover letter for a resume' WILL help you get a job.

My former principal, mentor, and very close friend Gary Mistovich had one mantra when it came to education. *Students don't care what you know until they know you care.* Period. As a teacher, I hope every student I've ever had will tell you that I cared about them. I tried to instill discipline, work ethic, responsibility, respect, and a love for learning. Speaking of Gary Mistovich, who we refer to as Misto, I can't continue here without adding a few things I was able to learn from him. We met as principal and teacher but quickly became close friends. He set an example each day for his students and teachers by the way he conducted himself. He never asked anyone in his building to do anything he wouldn't do himself. He told me once that you should always make sure your custodians and lunch room ladies know you care about them and that they're always taken care of. I never saw him talk down to a single employee – ever. During lunch each day, Misto would push the rolling trash can around by himself so students could throw their trays away. How many of you have ever seen a principal actually take up lunchroom trash each day? I'm not saying it doesn't happen, but it's definitely rare. It needed to be done so he did it. Once, while he was pushing the trash can around, a student accidentally threw her $300 retainer away. She didn't realize it until about an hour later after the bags had all been emptied into the dumpster out back. Gary Mistovich, the principal of the school, climbed into that dumpster and searched in the garbage, most of which was yucky thrown away food, for over an hour until he found that little girl's retainer. That's just what he did.

Another thing he told me was to always hire the best people possible and then get out of the way and let them do their jobs. He showed respect for everyone who worked for him, but was also not afraid to make tough decisions when needed. I could go on and on with stories and things I learned from him. I'm very thankful God put him in my life.

I developed many strong relationships with students over the years, but it seemed like the strongest relationships were built with the players I coached. When you spend 2-3 hours per day with a player for months and months, you develop a bond that's hard to duplicate in the classroom. As I said earlier, the best coaches were usually the best teachers, too. Coaching is teaching.

A story that sticks in my mind about coaching happened during my first year as the head football coach and head basketball coach at a newly opened school. Gary Mistovich was my new principal. We were not very competitive in athletics that year. In fact, we really only had one truly gifted male athlete in the entire school. Richard played football and basketball for me. He looked like he was at least 16 but had really only just turned 13. Tall, muscular, and strong. But Richard had a bit of a prima donna complex. He had always been the superstar in little league and was used to getting his way. It took some tough discipline for him to understand that although he was obviously more talented than anyone else on the field or court for us, he still had to follow the same rules as anyone else. At the beginning of basketball season, it was clear that Richard was the only hope we had of ever winning a game that year. So when he talked back and became extremely disrespectful to a teacher during class one day, I had a decision to make. We had a home game that day against the previous year's league champion. I knew that even with Richard in the lineup, we'd have a hard time competing. But if I allowed him to play, what kind of precedent was I setting for the rest of the team? There was only one answer. Richard would not be allowed to dress out or play in the game. He would have to sit on the bench in his shirt and tie and watch his teammates. He needed to learn that his poor behavior and choices in the classroom would have negative consequences.   I explained to him, in private, how disappointed I was in his behavior and that he would be suspended from playing in the game that day. He didn't like it, but knew me well enough to simply say yes sir and do as I ask. It's funny. We won three football championships in a row at that school and two basketball championships in a row while I was the head coach. But many people remember more the day I sat our best athlete out of a game because of poor choices he made. We, of course, lost the game by a zillion points, but I hope I taught Richard and our other players a valuable lesson that day. No matter who you are or what type of athlete you are, you must follow the rules just like anyone else. I've always told my players that I hold them to an even higher standard than students who didn't play sports. If you don't follow the rules and conduct yourself appropriately, you will be punished. I learned that most kids long for structure. Just like your own children at home, set the rules fairly for everyone and enforce them consistently for everyone. It ain't rocket science.

One last thing about coaching, I was a football and basketball coach for twelve years. As a head coach, I led our team in the Lord's Prayer before every single game I ever coached. Guess what? There was never a problem. No one ever complained. No parents called and asked for their player to be excluded. Our school wasn't threatened with any lawsuits. We just thanked the Lord for what we had, asked him to keep us and the other team safe, and played the game. I'm amazed and disgusted by the people who sue school districts today to keep coaches from leading their teams in prayer before and/or after games. This entire country was founded on Christian principles and faith. I, for one, refuse to turn my back on that. I have never nor would I ever force a player to pray with me. I've coached nearly a thousand players. Not one has ever declined to join me in the Lord's Prayer. Do not tell me I can't pray or set an example for my players.

When I left coaching and teaching to become an administrator, it was bittersweet. I loved teaching in the classroom, and I loved coaching my players. But after twelve years, I felt like it was time for me to proceed to the next step in my career. I've always said that I always want to be in the position where I can affect the most change. I was lucky enough to have worked for and learned from two great principals. Patsy Dean in Thomaston, GA and Gary Mistovich in Covington, GA. They each had completely different styles, but each was a fantastic leader whose work ethic was second to none.

As an assistant principal, I wanted to make sure everyone knew how much I cared about them and how much I loved my job. I tried to make sure my principal knew that I was loyal to her and had her back. I wanted my teachers and support staff to know that I cared about them and would do anything I could to make sure they had all they needed to succeed. I wanted them to know they always had my full support unless they did something I couldn't support. If that ever happened, I just asked that they let me know about it as soon as possible. If you accidentally told a student to shut up or got irate with a parent and maybe said something you should not have said, please let me know immediately. Don't let me get blindsided by a parent or the superintendent about an incident that occurred in our building. Another lesson I learned from my buddy Misto.

Also, as an assistant principal, I tried to do my "rounds" each morning and each afternoon. I tried to always make time twice a day to walk the entire school, sticking my head in classrooms just to say hi or even just wave. As an administrator, you find out very quickly who's doing what in your building if you make your rounds twice a day.

Teachers who worked at my school will tell you (I hope!) that my door was always open for them for whatever reason. A big part of my job was to make their jobs easier.

I could go on forever with stories about students, teachers, coaches, and administrators. Let's just summarize what I think are a few of the most important things I learned in my 17 years as a teacher, coach, and administrator:

1. Never assume anything about anybody or any given situation. Take the time to learn all the facts before making a decision.

2. Students, including your own children, want structure in their lives. Set fair rules, enforce those rules, and enforce the consequences when rules are

broken. All rules apply equally to all people.

3. No one cares what you know until they know you care. This applies at home, school, business, and church.

4. Always lead by example. Never ask those under you to do anything you wouldn't do yourself.

Chapter 17   Religion

It's amazing to me how easily people get all worked up when talking about religion. Especially here in the South. I'll be the first to tell you that I'm not the most religious person in the world. I didn't grow up going to church with my parents. In fact, the only times I ever remember seeing my parents in a church were at weddings, funerals, or baptisms. My parents taught us to pray and taught us the importance of God in our lives. We prayed as a family before each meal and at night before bed. At times, my brother and I would sometimes attend Sunday School when a bus would come around to get us. I remember going to Vacation Bible School in the summers, too. But we never regularly attended church as a family. My parents led what I think were very Christian lives, but actually attending church never interested them I guess.

So that's pretty much how I led my life too until my wife and I had our daughter Hannah. Even in my first marriage with my son Luke, I never had any real interest in attending church. I had nothing against it, but I just continued on the path my parents had started. We prayed and considered ourselves God-fearing Christians, but just never took it any further.

Several years after Hannah was born, my wife and I started talking about the importance of building a strong Christian foundation for her, and we both felt like that should include finding a church family.

We moved to Cordele, GA when Hannah was in kindergarten. After visiting several churches, we decided to join the First Baptist Church of Cordele. We felt very comfortable there, and Pastor Ray Sullivan was a young and energetic guy we liked a lot. FBC also had a great children's program, and Hannah jumped in immediately! From Awanas to church trips to vacation bible school, she got involved. My wife volunteered on several committees, and we attended church on Sundays on a pretty regular basis.

Flash forward several years to January of 2010 when my accident occurred. The importance of a church family became glaringly evident. Ray Sullivan traveled from

Cordele to Augusta several times to visit Joanna and pray over my bed where I lay in a coma. The church helped us with travel expenses, with Hannah, and whatever else Joanna needed. When something needed to be done at the house, the church made sure someone came over to repair or tighten or do whatever she needed.

When I woke from my coma, I can't explain the excitement I felt about my life and what I needed to do. I immediately told my wife about my horrible experience or dream or whatever it was of being in that cold, dark water at night and not being able to leave. I told her how scared I was that I would never see her or our children again and how hard I prayed and prayed and prayed. I told her how I promised God that I'd be a better Christian, father, and husband if he would just get me out of that horrible place and let me go back to my family. Somehow I knew at that moment, still lying in that hospital bed with tubes running everywhere and thousands of staples holding me together, that my future was going to include writing this book and becoming a motivational speaker. It's taken 5 ½ years, but here I go!

So you probably think that I'm going to tell you that I immediately started going to church every time the doors opened and sat in the front row waving my hands and singing God's praises to the world every chance I got, right? Not exactly. That's just not me. Not right now anyway.

We attend church on what I would call a semi-regular basis. Since moving back to my hometown of Fitzgerald nearly one year ago, we have visited several churches but still haven't decided on a permanent church home. I read my Bible every day. Not much on some days but still every day. We pray before meals and before bedtime every day. As a family, we regularly thank God for all of our blessings and ask that he bless those who are less fortunate.

Is that enough? We've all been baptized and accepted Jesus Christ as our Lord and Savior. We will eventually settle on a permanent church home, but even then, we will very rarely be there every single Sunday. I've heard others brag that they "haven't missed church on Sunday in more than three years." And that's fantastic – for them. More power to them and all other people like them. But, and this is a big but that many of you may not agree with (and that's ok, too), I do not believe for one second that anyone is a better Christian than I am simply because they attend church more times than me. I choose to believe that the God I serve doesn't have a rating system for Christians. Either you believe and have accepted Jesus Christ as your Lord and Savior or you do not and have not. I truly believe it is that simple.

I know (and so do you) many, many people who go to church for reasons other than getting closer to God. Some want to see who can out dress the other; some want to see who's not there just so they can talk about them at the beauty shop; and some just want to put on a show so they can act all holier than thou to everyone. The sad thing is that it's often those very people who are leading the most un-Christian like lives of all.

Please don't misunderstand my words. I am a faithful Christian and so are my wife and children. We try hard not to pass judgement on anyone. And I certainly don't mean to bash anyone for going to church every Sunday. We have many wonderful friends who are devout Christians who attend church every Sunday of their lives. I truly admire their faith and dedication. These are people who are there for the right reasons. My whole point is that I don't concern myself anymore with what others think of me.

Do you know who knows without a doubt that I am a faithful Christian man who loves God and prays and gives thanks to him every single day? My wife, my children, and my God. And it doesn't matter what anyone else thinks.

Now, after my near death experience, I definitely want to share my story and my faith with others. I honestly think that's why I'm still here. I think God wants me to share my life and experiences with others in order to make their lives better. And that's exactly what I'm going to do.

In closing this chapter on religion, please let me make one thing perfectly clear. Churches are amazing institutions. I know of many churches, pastors, and congregations who do amazing work in their respective communities. In no way am I saying you shouldn't go to church. But I am saying that just because you may go to church more times than me, that in itself doesn't make you any more of a Christian than I am.

In summary:

1. Don't judge others. It's just not your place.
2. Read your Bible daily. I find words to live by each time I open it.
3. Like my Daddy said, preach your funeral each day by the way you live your life – by the way you treat others, by the way you take care of your family, by the respect you show to your elders.
4. Pray before each meal and before bed each night. Teach your children to do the same.
5. Find a church where you and your family feel comfortable.
6. As always, in religion or any other facet of your life, try to

make your little part of the
world a better place.

Chapter 17

Jimmy and Carolyn Puckett - My Parents

My parents, Jimmy Puckett and
Carolyn McDonald Puckett, met in 7th grade.
They graduated from Fitzgerald High School
in 1963 and married on July 4, 1965. My
Daddy was a giant of a man. He was 6'3' and
usually around 280 lbs or so. He worked in
construction his entire life so his forearms
looked like Popeye's. He could drive a nail all
the way through a 2x4 with a flick of his
wrist. Daddy loved life, and he loved his
family.

My parents started "dating" in the
7th grade. We've always enjoyed hearing the

stories about their courtship over the years. Mama's family was definitely poorer than Daddy's. After all, Mama had three brothers and three sisters. Can you imagine having seven children? Joanna and often joke that it's all we can do just to keep up with the one child we still have at home. Daddy loved to joke that he bought Mama her first pair of real shoes. Mama just scoffed at him and laughed.

Daddy was quite the athlete, ladies' man, and rebel without a cause in high school. Apparently, Daddy had quite a few girlfriends in high school while Mama only had him. Daddy also got into his share of fights as a teen. This is something he would be totally embarrassed about later in life. It seems that even as an adult when we moved back to Fitzgerald, some idiot rednecks were always trying to start a fight to prove they could "whip Jimmy Puckett." Well, that never worked out well. I've never had a man say a negative word to me about my Daddy. I remember one man saying to me, "Jim, I never saw your Daddy start a fight in all the years I knew him...But I saw him end plenty of them."

Daddy was a smart man, too. Although you'd apparently never know it from his academic exploits or lack thereof in school. Two stories stand out to me. One involved Mama's senior yearbook. At the top of one of the pages, she had written "Reserved for Jimmy." I don't remember all that he wrote, but I do remember that he took up the whole page. The best (or worst?) line of his writing to his future wife was "Thank you so much for doing all of that homework for me. I never would have gotten through school without you." Why on Earth, even if that were true, would you write that in a yearbook knowing people would see those words for years and years to come? Not real bright, Daddy. We gave him a very hard time about those words each time we started looking through the yearbooks. Of course, he denied the allegations even though it was right there in his own handwriting!

The other story happened years later when I was a freshman in college at the University of Georgia. I arrived home one weekend on a Friday afternoon and walked in the house. Daddy was standing in the kitchen with his head kind of bowed down into his hands. I startled him, and he quickly wiped away a few tears from his eyes. Now understand that to this point in my life, I do not remember ever seeing my Daddy cry. Ever. So I was completely taken aback and had no idea what to say. I just said, "Are you okay?" He kind of shook his head and laughed a little and said, "Yeah, I'm fine." I'm just an idiot sometimes." Now I was really confused. My Daddy wasn't much of a talker or a man who shared his feelings with anyone. So to my surprise, he continued and told me what had happened to him the night before. Sometimes after he closed our restaurant at night, he would go by the local Huddle House and sit at the counter and have a few cups of coffee before heading home. It was his way of winding down after a long day. On this particular night, an old high school nemesis had been there when Daddy arrived. If I said his name, many of you Fitzgerald folks would know exactly who I'm talking about. The guy was drunk and kind of playfully started messing with Daddy. He was saying things like "Oooh, it's big bad Jimmy Puckett!" among other things. Just being an ignorant and annoying drunk. Daddy told him several times to go on and leave him alone, but the guy wouldn't let it go. He finally said the wrong thing one too many times, and Daddy knocked him out in the floor with one punch. Daddy then paid for his coffee and went home and went to bed.

The next day Daddy received a phone call from the high school athletic director letting him know that he might want to make sure that he and Mama were at the high school gym later that afternoon. They were giving out athletic awards, and my brother Wayne was going to be receiving the top athletic award in the school. He had also just put my brother on restriction because he and my cousin Danny had lied to him earlier in the week when they had skipped school to go out of town to reserve a limousine for the prom. They told Mama what they were doing but knew Daddy would never go for them skipping any classes for anything. Which is rather ironic considering his academic prowess in high school. But I digress... My Daddy always told us that no matter what we did in life, we had better never lie to him about anything. So when my brother told what he thought was a harmless, little white lie, especially since Mama knew about it, he never expected to be put on restriction for it. I forgot exactly how Daddy found out, but it wasn't pretty.

So...all this leads to me finding Daddy wiping tears from his face in the kitchen. It turns out that he was upset because here he was, in his mind doing the right thing by punishing my brother for lying to him, and then he gets the phone call about him receiving this big award AND after always preaching to us about doing the right thing, he goes and knocks a man out the night before in the Huddle House. Almost sounds like the beginning of a country song! I think he was just really embarrassed by what he'd done. I just told him that we loved him and respected him and that the reason all three of us were like we were was because of the respect and responsibility he always demanded from us. I don't think I ever saw him cry again.

I could write an entire book on Daddy. He died on April 30, 1989. He had a car accident on April 1, 1989. I'll never forget that date because he had asked me to go with him that night. He asked me to ride down to the river with him. I'll never forget what I said to him. I said, "Daddy, I can go with you anytime. The Final Four basketball games are on tonight, and I want to stay and watch them." He said ok and that he'd see me tomorrow. A police officer knocked on our door sometime that night, and told us Daddy had been in a wreck.

The next four weeks were a blur. I was in my senior year at UGA and couldn't afford to miss a lot of school. My brother Wayne was a freshman baseball player at South Georgia College in Douglas, and my sister Susie was only 12. We all practically lived in the ICU waiting room at the Tifton Hospital in Tifton, GA. Not to mention my Mama had a restaurant to run six days a week.

Daddy had drifted into a coma for the last two weeks of his life. We would go into see him, but we didn't know if he knew we were there. But on April 29th, the most amazing thing happened. Daddy woke up. He was awake and alert the entire day. He couldn't speak, but he would mouth the words "I love you" to us and even wrote words on paper when he wanted to communicate. He was smiling and seemed in great spirits. We all stayed in the room with him nearly all day. It was one of the best days of my life actually.

After sleeping all night in the waiting room, which is what we did most nights, I went in to see Daddy before leaving to get some breakfast the next morning. I remember his eyes being wide open, almost as if he was fighting to keep them open. His hands gripped the side of the bed as tightly as he could. We didn't really think anything of it after the great day we had the day before. We all kissed him and told him we loved him and that we were going to get some breakfast.

Upon returning to the hospital after breakfast, the nurse immediately told us that the doctor wanted to see us. We were ushered into a room, and one of Daddy's doctors told us he had passed away. If this had happened two days earlier, we would have all expected it. But after the fantastic day he had yesterday? After he awoke from a coma and spent the entire day with us, joking and talking? We were shocked to say the least. You just never get prepared enough for one of your parents to die. He was only 43. The older I get, the more I realize just how young he was.

To this day, I truly believe that God allowed Daddy to wake up for that last day so that we would always have the memories of spending that day together, happy, as a family. I also believe that Daddy fought all that next night to stay awake and alive just so he could see us all one more time. I think that's why he looked as if he were fighting to keep his eyes open and why he was gripping the sides of the bed so tightly. After we all kissed him and said goodbye as were going to breakfast, I think he felt it was finally okay to let go. He was tired of fighting. God, I loved that man so much.

I told you before how Daddy always said that a man preaches his own funeral every day of his life. Well, Daddy apparently did a lot of preaching because his funeral was one of the largest ever held at our local funeral home in Fitzgerald. People from all over Georgia sent so many flowers that they filled two extra rooms in addition to the room where Daddy lay. It was crazy! I met SO many people whose lives had been affected in a positive way by Daddy. One man about 25 years old came up to me and said, "Jim, you don't know me, but your Dad helped me and my family out more than he'll ever know. You see, he was a member of the Lion's Club, and my wife is a waitress at the steakhouse where they had their weekly meetings. They were talking, and my wife mentioned that I had lost my job recently. Your Dad asked to meet me. He made a phone call, got me a good job, and even gave us a little money until I received my first paycheck. I will never forget what he did for my family, and I just wanted to share that with you."

Wow! He was definitely not the only person who shared their thoughts and memories of Daddy with us over the next few days and weeks. His funeral, as sad as it obviously was, was truly a celebration of his great life.

It's been 26 years now since Daddy passed away, and I still think about him nearly every day. He was a larger than life man in my eyes, and I'm so thankful he was my Daddy. He taught me how to be a man, a husband, and a father by the way he lived his life each day.

So now I get to tell you more about the most amazing woman I've ever met. Carolyn Faye McDonald Puckett – my Mama!

Mama is now 70 years young. I say young because anyone who knows her knows that she doesn't look her age nor act it. Mama doesn't drink or smoke and never has.

I don't even know where to begin to tell you about this awesome woman and the tremendous upbringing she provided for my sister, brother, and me. She is without a doubt the strongest woman I've ever known. When Daddy died in 1989, she became a widow with a married son still in college, another son in his freshman year at college, and a twelve year old daughter. After Daddy's funeral, people would ask me, "Is your Mama going to keep Johnnie's open?" Johnnies Drive In was the hometown restaurant Daddy had taken over a few years before his death. I had to laugh at that question because Mama pretty much ran Johnnie's already. Daddy like to ride around and act like a bigshot with a little money in his pocket, but it was Mama who made sure Johnnie's kept going each day. People seem to think owning a restaurant means you are very wealthy. If they only knew! Johnnie's brought in a lot of business, but it's a very expensive operation to run each day, as well.

So, from a few weeks after Daddy died in 1989 until just a few months ago on July 27, 2015, Mama ran Johnnie's. She was at Johnnie's making coffee and cooking up breakfast by 4:30 AM six days a week. She usually worked until 2:00 and then went home for a nap. That was her schedule for nearly 26 years! Think about that. 9 ½ hour days that start at 4:30 in the morning six days a week. She closed on Christmas Day, Thanksgiving, and always closed the week of July 4th. That's it. I can count on two hands the days she has ever missed work. And only then because she had extremely severe back pain that flared up occasionally. Even then, if she could walk and pop enough pain medication, she'd be in the kitchen at Johnnie's doing her thing. Cooking the best homemade food in town and taking care of people.

Johnnie's was such a special place. It's hard to explain, but it was just like home to most people. Mama would be there by herself from 4:30 AM until about 8:00 AM Monday – Saturday. Being by herself, she had to stay in the kitchen most of the time. There was a server's window open to the dining area, and that's where most people would just stick their head through and tell Mama what they wanted for breakfast. Some would come into the kitchen to get their morning hug or just to say good morning. When someone wanted coffee, they got up, got the pot, and walked around filling everyone else's cup as well.

There was a large table that could sit eight people in the center of the dining area at Johnnie's. That's where most everyone sat at breakfast if they got there early enough. Someone coined it "the table

of knowledge" and it stuck. Each day, all of
our regulars could be heard at that table
solving the world's problems. They could tell
you who should be our President and why,
what play the football coach should have
called last night, and who was sleeping with
who. They knew it all! Honestly, I used to
absolutely love sitting at breakfast with all
those folks. Mama usually knew what they
wanted for breakfast before they even sat
down because most were there every single
day and always had the same thing. If she
got caught up in the kitchen, she might come
out and say hey to everyone or give 'em hell
for whatever they were saying about her.
They all loved to cut up with Mama, and the
back and forth banter was too funny! When
customers got ready to pay their bill, most
just went and put their money in the open
cash register and got change if needed. Yes, I
said that most mornings at Johnnie's Drive In,
Mama trusted people just to pay their own
tabs by putting their money into the open

cash register. She was usually busy cooking. Do any of you know of another restaurant like that today? She even had people who would bring their own special sausage or other meat for her to cook them for breakfast. She'd cook it right up and still charge them, too. She had one longtime customer who nearly every morning liked to come in the kitchen and cook his own breakfast! One day I said, "Mama, so this man brings his own food and cooks it himself and you still charge him for it?" Without missing a beat, she replied, "Yes siree!"

And if you brought children into Johnnie's, you'd better make them behave or Mama would do it for you. She had no problem disciplining anyone's children if they were acting a fool or being disrespectful in her restaurant. She just didn't put up with it – period.

Mama is 70 years old now and healthy as a horse. She is just a special,

special lady, and I thank God each day that she is my mother. She taught me work ethic, responsibility, and respect. She, as a 43 old widow, busted her tail and put three kids through college by herself. She never complained about anything. She just got up each day and did whatever needed to be done to take care of her family.

CHAPTER 18   Other Stuff

This last chapter before I wrap things up is going to include just mostly random thoughts that pop into my head that maybe I haven't covered anywhere else in the book. Some useful; some maybe not. You can judge.

1. Twelve year olds should NOT have a Facebook page.
2. PLEASE use correct grammar when posting anything on social

media so I don't think you're an idiot.

3. Guys – if you have to hold your pants up while you walk to keep them from falling down around your ankles, you're an idiot. You don't look cool or hip or anything else except stupid. Buy pants that fit your waist and wear a belt.

4. When using social media, stop complaining and whining about your horrible life just to get attention. It makes you appear weak and pathetic.

5. When driving, use your blinkers please.

6. Kiss your spouse every single day.

7. Say thank you.

8. Open doors for women and the elderly.

9. Do not get in the fast lane unless you plan to drive ABOVE the speed limit.

10. Exercise daily. I don't care if it's just a walk around the block, get up and get outside and MOVE.

11. Encourage your children to play sports. They will learn about work ethic, responsibility, team work, and much more.

12. Do NOT take infants or toddlers to weddings or funerals. That's what babysitters are for. If you absolutely have to do so, be respectful and leave IMMEDIATELY if your child starts crying.

13. No matter your situation in life, your attitude makes all the difference in the world.

14. Save money, and buy as little as possible on credit.

15. If you are going to be late paying a bill, call the creditor and tell them.
16. Guys – Do not wear crocs – ever.
17. Read something every single day of your life.
18. Never stop learning.
19. Be very careful of who you trust in this world.
20. Talk to your parents and siblings and children every day if possible.
21. Turn your phone OFF when you're in a movie theater.
22. Always keep the oil changed regularly in your vehicle.
23. Insurance is important. Make sure you and your family have enough.
24. Be an honest person.
25. When you tell someone you're going to do something, do it.

Chapter 19   Wrap it Up!

On January 16, 2010 I died in a Medivac helicopter that was transporting me to Doctor's Hospital in Augusta, GA. I died. My heart stopped pumping blood, and my lungs stopped breathing oxygen. I was 42 years old and because of a stupid mistake, I was leaving my family to fend for themselves in this world. My wife Joanna, son Luke, and daughter Hannah would have to take care of themselves from now on. They were going to have to plan a funeral and bury me and go through all the heart wrenching agony that occurs when a Dad and husband dies suddenly, tragically, and much too young.

Except that's not the end of the story. God sent me back. He sent me back to my family. He gave me a second chance. My near-death experience was not a happy one.

I didn't see any bright white lights with previously deceased family members waiting for me at the end of a tunnel. I didn't hear angels singing or trumpets blaring, welcoming me to the Pearly Gates. No. Instead, I was put into a fence in some deep, dark water with a bunch of other people who didn't want to be there. It was a horrible, menacing place, and there was no way out. But I found a way. I found a way back to my family through prayer. When I found myself in that water, I prayed like I had never prayed before. I promised God that if he would just let me go back to my family, I would be a better man, a better Christian, a better father, and a better husband. And sometime after that, I woke up in the hospital after a two month coma.

Now...did I really die and go to Hell? I have no idea. Is my entire memory just a hallucinogenic dream brought about by all the drugs I was being given? I don't know that either. It's definitely a possibility. What I do know is that I never want to go in that dark water again. What I do know is that I promised God that I would be a better man if he allowed me to go back to my family, and he DID!

Since waking up in that hospital, I AM a better man. You'll have to ask my wife and children if I'm a better husband and father, but I think I know their answers. And I know without a doubt I've been a better Christian. I read my Bible more. I attend church more. I give my testimony to all who will listen. And I'm about to give a whole lot more!

Please don't take anything I've said in this book as me thinking I'm better or smarter than you or thinking I have all the answers. God led me to share my story and experiences with you to help you. If anything I've shared in this book leads you to become a better person in any way, then I'm good with that.

I'll leave you with this....ALWAYS TRY TO MAKE YOUR LITTLE PIECE OF THE WORLD A BETTER PLACE. Think about the possibilities if we all do that. Just stop worrying about everyone else and just make your little piece of the world better.

And lastly, please don't ever put gasoline on a fire. Just not a good idea!

<u>Acknowledgments</u>

First and foremost, I must thank my God. He brought me back for a reason, and I'm trying to do right by his decision. Thank you to my wife Joanna. None of this would be possible without you. After being a stay at home mom for seven years, you went back into the work force to allow me to chase this dream of becoming an author and motivational speaker. You are my rock, and I still fall in love with you more each day. Thank you to my wonderful children, Luke and Hannah. You both make me so proud to be your Dad. Thank you to my Mama, Carolyn Puckett Chambers for being an inspiration to me every day of my life. You are amazing. Thank you to my brother Wayne Puckett and sister Susie Salinas. I treasure the close relationship we are so fortunate to have more than you can possibly know.

Others I need to thank are my best friend Tim Frost and his wife Diane, my cousin/brother Danny Smith, Don Adkins, Rob Garber (a friend and fellow educator who once stated that I should get at least a 50% discount on cremation when I die since I've already done half the job!), and many, many more! Durwood Helms, James Peek, Gary Mistovich, Paul McSwain, Stewart Carswell, Hank Braddy along with just about every educator I've ever known. Thank you to the heroes on the Medivac helicopter out of Cordele, GA. I simply would not be here today without you. Thank you to Sherry Videtto, Augusta Burn Center Outreach Coordinator, who befriended my family and did everything possible to make sure they were comfortable and had everything they needed during my stay. Thank you to all of the amazing medical staff at the Joseph M. Still Burn Center in Augusta, GA. From nurses to doctors to therapists and everyone in between, you are without a doubt the most professional and dedicated medical professionals I have ever had the pleasure to know. Thank you Mr. Jack McKinley, Dr. Charles Lewis, and Brenda Parks Whitley – high school teachers who inspired me to write back at Fitzgerald High School.

Anyone interested in having me speak to your organization, please contact me at jimpuckett1967@gmail.com. I promise I will not be boring!